Writers of Wales

EDITORS

MEIC STEPHENS   R. BRINLEY JONES

E. TEGLA DAVIES

1880-1967

Pennar Davies

E. TEGLA

DAVIES

University of Wales Press
on behalf of the Welsh Arts Council

1983

I

The poet-preacher in Welsh-speaking Wales in the last century is a phenomenon not strictly paralleled elsewhere, though it is not difficult to think of literary clerics in many ages and lands. Edward Tegla Davies is not among the poet-preachers: he had no pretensions to any mastery over verse forms and his limpid prose nowhere shows any sign of poetic afflatus, not quite even in his TIR Y DYNEDDON *(The Land of Little Men)*. But he was equally distinguished as preacher and as writer and refused to dissociate his two vocations. Literary recognition meant much to him. He himself tells us how a word of generous praise from Idris Bell lifted him up on unseen wings to heaven and how a disillusioning word of adverse criticism from Saunders Lewis drew him down to hell. This was partly because he had not received the kind of education which might be considered appropriate for a Welsh literary figure and had begun to write in a creative way only after being invited to contribute a story serially to a religious magazine for children. He never felt entirely sure of himself. But there was also the fact that he consciously subordinated his literary art to his supreme concern as *'minister of the Gospel'*—the bald description of him on the stone at his grave in Tre-garth—and that this laid him open to the charge, only partly true but none the less wholly unanswerable, that as an artist he lacked the integrity which even his severest critics admitted that he had as a man of God. Among twentieth-century Welsh writers who have left behind them some works which are likely to remain classics he is surely one of unique interest.

He has given us a valued book of reminiscences, GYDA'R BLYNYDDOEDD *(With the Years),* and this has been put to good use by Huw Ethall in his TEGLA, in which the biographical spade work has been more than adequately done. An outline of his life can be attempted with some confidence.

Edward Tegla Davies was born on 31 May 1880 to one of the poorest families in the declining country district of Llandegla. The middle name *Tegla* was adopted by Edward Davies later on, a frequent expedient among the Welsh whose unfortunate history has left them with a number of surnames which are so common that they fail to identify those whom they label. Tegla is the saint commemorated in the place name *Llandegla,* the original Saint Thecla being the apocryphal lady of Iconium who was converted to Christianity and especially to Christian virginity by Paul. Among our Tegla's forbears the most memorable are his hard-drinking and hard-fighting paternal grandfather and his maternal grandmother, the erring daughter of a well-to-do family who married beneath her station. His parents were William and Mary Ann Davies, both of them loved and respected by Tegla. Neither had had any schooling. The father could write only a little and the mother not at all but both could read and the few books, all in Welsh, that were in the house were well thumbed. Tegla remembered the washed sugar sacking that covered the earth floor—and put it into his novel GŴR PEN Y BRYN *(The Master of Hilltop Farm)*. The family moved house several times. They were humbly devout and faithful to the Wesleyan cause and belonged to a rural community in which the only riches were the Welsh speech and the evangelical faith and in which a shy lad could meet the eccentric Ehedydd Iâl, the author of the most dramatic single verse of a hymn ever written even in Welsh.

At the age of five the boy was pitched into an alien world: school. There the three Rs were taught with utilitarian exclusiveness, and they were English reading, English writing and English arithmetic. It was only in an accidental way that the boys learnt to their surprise that the schoolmaster could speak Welsh after all. Transference to another school in another area at the age of twelve brought no relief, for the new headmaster dutifully and savagely persecuted the native language in his domain. Edward Davies was grateful to his Sunday school and to an admirable teacher there. He was also glad of his home and was deeply attached to those of his brothers and sisters who were near to him in age and especially to his sister Hannah. He was a sickly child in his early years and his head would often be tightly bound with a cloth to ease oppressive headaches. He had a moral sensitivity which ensured that throughout his life he was to be troubled with

3

childhood memories of sins which were partly accidents—half killing a cat out of terror with a poker, killing a blue tit by casually throwing a stone in its direction. His memories of the sound of killer dogs attacking sheep at night remained with him to find their place in his novel. His delicate health and his gifts of intellect were inevitably a problem in so miserably poor a family in which children had to leave home at a tender age to become the servants of their betters. A bitter memory was the closing of the Foel Faen quarry which put his father temporarily out of work when Edward was about seven years old. A solution to the problem of the boy's future seemed to offer itself when at the age of fourteen he was dignified by the formidable headmaster with the amphibious and ambivalent office of 'pupil teacher'. It turned out to be a form of slave labour but this did not prevent him from showing promise and even originality as an educator.

When he was about seventeen his horizons were excitingly extended. The radical Welsh Liberalism represented by Tom Ellis, Lloyd George and Thomas Gee seemed to many a young Welshman to promise a new heaven and a new earth. In a local election meeting held in 1897 he heard the three of them speak with effect and the enthusiasm was such that a hopeful youth might be pardoned for believing that the millennium was at hand. Tegla spoke of it later in terms of disillusionment not untouched (when he considered the subsequent fortunes of the candidate) by cynicism. A more substantial blessing was the coming of a new and young teacher to his school at Bwlch-gwyn, Tom Arfor Davies. To Edward

Davies his impact was a *'miracle'*. Handsome, affable, courteous, interested in his work and his pupils, he changed the tone of the school by speaking Welsh as if it were the most natural thing in the world. He introduced Edward to the work of O. M. Edwards and to a shop which sold Welsh books. Passing completely under O.M.'s spell the youth wrote a story with a temperance moral and had the satisfaction of seeing it in print in O.M.'s magazine CYMRU. He tried his hand even at verse and a poem of his about love and parting appeared in Y FANER in 1899. Another commitment was his venturing to preach about three months after Tom Arfor's coming to Bwlch-gwyn. His pilgrimage to the pulpit had begun under the transporting experience of the rare eloquence of John Evans, Eglwys-bach, two or three years previously. No doubt the lad's inner motivation had been mixed, the genuine piety of his upbringing having been stirred to new life and the desire to serve touched with the desire to sway and captivate an audience. A year or so after this he had heard Ben Davies, Pant-teg, urging young people to read the Bible from cover to cover. This he had done and after finishing the last chapter of Revelation had felt the urge to preach the marvels of which he had read. Something like a conversion had followed soon afterwards: hearing J. P. Roberts in a week of preaching in his chapel and then feeling that he was being hunted by hounds, rushing away until he reached a place which commanded a lovely view of the border country and gazing at it under the stars until he felt the tranquillity of the scene mingling with an inner peace. There followed his reception as church member and eventually (with but little encouragement from the local church leaders who looked for gifts of utterance which they felt he lacked) his beginning to preach.

Speaking of what we may call his conversion experience Tegla says that the horrendous feeling of being pursued by hounds did not arise out of fear of punishment but sprang rather from a despairing sense of his own unworthiness. He seems to mean what the theology of evangelism calls a conviction of sin, but he does not specify. Of his ethical sensitivity there can be no doubt and it is not difficult to imagine what the emotional stresses of a late Victorian adolescent may have been. What is interesting is that in his description of the process of finding inward peace it is the beauty and tranquillity of a lovely view at eventide that brings soothing and wholeness while the evangelical doctrines are not mentioned. It is equally interesting to note that he confesses that his first sermon was lifted from the work of John Jones, Tal-sarn, and that he tried for some years to impress his hearers with two devices, the singing *hwyl* and story illustrations, for neither of which he had any aptitude. He seems also to have had very little difficulty in shedding the literalist approach to the Bible. A word from Tom Arfor Davies was enough to convince him that the stories of the Creation and the Fall and the Flood were poetry rather than history and that to recognise this in no way involved a rejection of the faith. All this means that he was still seeking his path. In no sense was he consciously breaking with the evangelical tradition. He felt that he was truly ordained when Ehedydd Iâl looked into his eyes and put his hands on his shoulders and told him to preach, after becoming a minister, on the last sentence in Ezekiel.

After two years of lay preaching he became a candidate for the Wesleyan Methodist ministry and according to the requirements in those days had to have a year's practical experience of ministerial work before entering college. This year, 1901–2, he spent in the Llanasa circuit in Flintshire; and he was sad to leave it to become one of the seven Welsh students among the ninety who received instruction at Didsbury College, Manchester. His exile there was made the more distasteful by the gross self-importance of the College Principal whose two chief gods—so Tegla afterwards recorded—were himself and John Wesley the founder of '*Mthdsm*'; but there were compensations, especially the privilege of studying under the guidance of the gentle James Hope Moulton, a man of prodigious scholarship in the field of New Testament Greek. In Manchester Tegla scarcely heard more than echoes of the Welsh Revival of 1904–5; later he was to subject it to damaging criticism. Little of what he learnt in college was helpful to him as he faced his life work but he was more than amply compensated in 1905 when he spent some time assisting an ailing minister at Abergele, Evan Jones, whom he considered to be the greatest man he had ever met. He was not, of course, applying the standards of the world, and when he wrote his tribute he italicised the Welsh word for 'man'.

A happy year at Noddfa, Leeds, followed, and

7

then in 1907 Tegla—his adopted name was already in use—moved to Porthaethwy (Menai Bridge) in Anglesey, and soon he drew vials of wrath upon his head by condemning the sexual promiscuity and indeed prostitution which, he had been shocked to observe, was one of the by-products of the merriment of the town's famous annual fair. He got little support from his fellow-ministers and laid himself open to public rebuke; but was able to make use of the unpleasant experience later on in his portrayal of the ineffectual minister T. Cefnllech Roberts in his novel. Tegla was not the first or the last young minister to set himself up as a local Savonarola. His moral judgements were black and white and this must have been apparent in an early novel which he wrote in this period for a competition in the Anglesey eisteddfod of 1908—the only time he ever seriously competed apart from little efforts at Bwlch-gwyn. Although this work won the honours of the competition Tegla in later life condemned it as supercilious and sentimental. It seems that the wicked characters were very wicked and the good ones very good. But the literary urge had reawakened in him and another side of his character came into play in a series of pseudonymous letters written by him and a college friend to a denominational magazine to poke a little satire at the denominational mandarins. The series was terminated under pressure but Tegla was invited to contribute regular articles on religious affairs. This he did under a pseudonym and in colloquial Welsh which aroused sharp criticism from his purist friend D. Tecwyn Evans who did not know who the author was.

In 1908, on 19 August, he married Jane Eleanor
Evans, daughter of a Bwlch-gwyn shopkeeper and
lay preacher. He had met her just before Easter
1899 not without the help of Tom Arfor Davies
and from that first meeting there had been warm
mutual understanding. While making due allow-
ance for the pietistic flavour of any domestic
allusions in biographies and autobiographies of
pastors and preachers we can readily believe that
the partnership between Tegla and his wife was
uncommonly close and enriched by a shared
faith. Tegla afterwards testified that Bwlch-gwyn
had come to mean for him the love between him
and his wife and the friendship between him and
Tom Arfor Davies whose early death in 1901 had
been a sore loss to him and to Wales. When the
young minister and his wife left Anglesey for
Y Felinheli (Port Dinorwig) in September 1910,
they brought with them their baby girl Dyddgu.

Their stay at Y Felinheli was short, just about a
year; but he called it 'the fateful year' of his life—
an over-dramatic but revealing remark. In fairness
it must be said that he added the qualifying phrase
'in one sense'. It was the year in which he was
invited to contribute to Y WINLLAN (*The Vineyard*),
the Welsh Wesleyan monthly for children, and
produced anonymously the serial which, by no
means welcomed at the time by many of the
self-importantly religious, became the first of his
little classics, HUNANGOFIANT TOMI (*Tommy's
Memoirs*). It was published in book form in 1912.

Tegla with his family had already moved in
August 1911 to minister to the quarrymen of
Tre-garth. There he made a great friend of Ifor

Williams, then a young lecturer at Bangor, and gave hospitality to the Macwyaid ('squires', in the chivalric associations of the word), a short-lived group of youngish writers of the academic 'renaissance' in Welsh literature. They included R. Williams Parry, Elidir Sais (W. H. Jones) and Ifor Williams. Another interest, shared with Tecwyn Evans, was the promotion of modern critical methods in the understanding of the Bible. Under the joint editorship of Tecwyn and Tegla a collection of studies by a number of young authors was published under the title LLESTRI'R TRYSOR (*Treasure Vessels*) in 1913 and in spite, or rather because, of strong official opposition it sold well. At what must have been a particularly busy time Tegla was also called to the temporary editorship of the venerable Welsh Wesleyan periodical YR EURGRAWN (*The Golden Treasury*) while the former editor Dr. Hugh Jones busied himself with a bulky history of Welsh Wesleyanism which Tegla had to read and re-read, correct and re-correct in manuscript and in proof. As a preacher he was still not sure of his gifts and limitations but after a disastrous attempt to imitate Gipsy Smith (whom he heard in 1914) he came to learn to be himself. It was at Tre-garth that his son Arfor was born.

His removal to his next ministerial charge, the delectable region around Llanrhaeadr-ym-Mochnant, roughly synchronized with the out-break of the First World War. Soon after came the birth of his third child Gwenfyl. He was already developing near-pacifist views and could find little that was glorious in the costly conflict. But sometimes, among the delights of Llanrhaeadr

and his young family, he could feel that the war
was far away. He also found more than satisfaction
in literary creation. He contributed serially to
Yr Eurgrawn his ambitious and notable novel
Gŵr Pen y Bryn in which he drew upon his
memories and derived much local colour from
the countryside around Llanrhaeadr and Llandegla to garnish his tale of a soul in crisis. This
was in 1915–16. In 1917 the freezing of the marvellous waterfall Pistyll Rhaeadr inspired him to
contribute a more assured masterpiece, his Tir
y Dyneddon (*Land of Little Men*), little appreciated
at the time by the magazine's readers but destined
to be acclaimed by reputable critics on its appearance in book form in 1921.

It was during the war years that his great friendship with the poet T. Gwynn Jones began. He had
seen him from afar in the 1908 Eisteddfod. He
visited him with a mutual friend towards the
end of 1916 and in the Birkenhead Eisteddfod of
1917 they were together in the Gorsedd of the
Bards (Tegla having newly accepted the honour
of membership under persuasion 'for the sake of
the denomination') when the winner of the
Chair turned out to be the young poet Hedd
Wyn who had been killed in action at Pilkem
Ridge. The occasion was a perfect opportunity
for Lloyd George's magniloquent war-waging
oratory. Tegla and T. Gwynn Jones found that
they shared a disgust with the militaristic and
imperialistic flavour of the proceedings—a lamen-
table show from which poor Hedd Wyn's repu-
tation in critical quarters has never fully re-
covered. Though greatly drawn to Gwynn
Tegla was still troubled by the testimony (internal

11

and external) that the celebrated writer was an unbeliever but later, in November, when Tegla welcomed him to Llanrhaeadr and ventured the remark that the war had led many people to unbelief, there came the unexpected reply that the war had made the speaker a Christian. T. Gwynn Jones's real beliefs, before and after the war, have been much discussed since, but this confession in 1917 sealed a lifelong friendship with Gwynn Jones and his wife. On the question of war and peace Tegla at first, though abhorring the cruelty of war on moral grounds, wondered whether a war in defence of small countries and a war for Christianity and civilisation and a war to put an end to war could perhaps be justified. So his friend David Thomas has reported. But Tegla soon came to be sure that war could not bring about any of these benefits. He gave support to Y DEYRNAS (*The Kingdom*), a courageous weekly edited by Thomas Rees in furtherance of Christian pacifism, and was one of the contributors.

His return to the Tre-garth circuit in August 1919 brought him mixed feelings: sorrow at leaving beloved friends, pleasure in renewing cherished relationships and grievous disappointment at the decline of interest in matters of religious import, a decline shared with most other areas and due to the impact of the war. In 1920 he undertook the editorship of Y WINLLAN and began to contribute to it a new serial for children which was published in 1922 as a book under the title NEDW (*Neddy*). This told entertaining stories of a mischievous boy and showed a Dickensian flair for oddities. Some of his readers were moved to criticize the author for offering mere entertainment and neglecting his duty to provide moral edification. This complaint could scarcely be lodged against the only play Tegla ever wrote, MARY, a sentimental and moralizing piece about the deaths of an old couple and a prodigal son welcomed back by his sister, a work promptly forgotten after its unpromising appearance in 1920. During his nine years as editor of Y WINLLAN he opened its pages to contributors of note outside the Wesleyan fold. In 1920 and 1921 he found time to write pseudonymous articles to the literary magazine Y GENHINEN (*The Leek*), one of them repudiating an insinuation that some ministers were unduly concerned about making money and the other satirising an unworthy minister glorified with the name 'y Parch. J. Pwlpudedig Jones'. Before leaving Tre-garth for Denbigh in 1922 he had had the satisfaction of seeing his TIR Y DYNEDDON published as a volume and the intoxication—the word is not too strong—of the beginnings of a spate of critical acclaim which recognised its author as an outstanding literary artist while finding in it profundities which he had never intended.

His stay at Denbigh lasted until 1925 and was a time of trials, perplexities and disappointments. While he was much comforted in one of the churches he served, another, enjoying superior prestige, was, he found, tainted by snobbery and worldliness and more than ready to accept anglicization. He suffered grievous ill health. He was bewildered by political developments in Wales and by refusing to commit himself laid himself open to the charge of shirking leadership.

But he had one experience which brought into his preaching a new note of certainty. The condition of his eyes one evening brought him the sudden fear that he would lose his sight and drove him to agonized prayer. He heard a voice speaking with perfect clarity and saying words which had given comfort to Paul, 'My grace is sufficient for thee: for my strength is made perfect in weakness'. Tegla came to date his recovery from that moment and to testify that his preaching then lost its former cleverness and became confidently affirmative. Between 1922 and 1924 he produced booklets on Biblical personalities, while his literary standing was raised by the publication of NEDW and GŴR PEN Y BRYN in illustrated editions in 1922 and 1923. Likewise, his re-telling of the Grail stories in Y GREAL SANCTAIDD *(The Holy Grail)*, and of the tale of Branwen in BRANWEN FERCH LLŶR *(Branwen daughter of Llŷr)*, though too moralistic and marred by a style suggestive of a too earnest preacher talking down to children, added to his prestige in some quarters after their publication in 1922 and 1923. In 1924 he contributed to Y LLENOR *(The Writer)*, the premier Welsh literary organ, a satirical 'biography' of the ministerial fraud 'J. Pwlpudedig Jones' but once again sought refuge in a pseudonym. Perhaps this was just as well, for if it had been common knowledge that Tegla was the author of this damaging caricature of the conventional pietistic ministerial memoir there might have been angry murmurings against the conferment upon Tegla by the University of Wales of the honorary degree of M.A. in that same year.

In 1925 Tegla found himself assigned to Man-

14

chester and the change brought a renewal of
health and energy. The heaviness of the Manchester air delivered him from insomnia; the
water, much softer than that of the Denbigh
area, cured him of other ills; and the rush of
activities left him no time for melancholy
broodings. Fortunately they did not prevent him
from writing serially another literary *tour de force*
for children, Rhys Llwyd y Lleuad *(Grey Rhys of
the Moon)*, which duly came out as a book before
the end of the year: not quite a specimen of
science fiction but a combination of fantasy and
facts about the moon. About this same time he
tried to defend his abstention from party politics
in an article in Y Genhinen by accusing Welsh
Nonconformity of losing its vision by embracing
a political creed. He seems also to have abstained
from any public comments on the rights and
wrongs of the 1926 Strike. In that year his natural
self-esteem as a literary man of growing repu-
tation suffered a reeling blow when Saunders
Lewis briefly examined his work in his lecture
An Introduction to Contemporary Welsh
Literature. The severity with which the novel
Gŵr Pen y Bryn was handled astounded and
disturbed Tegla who found himself accused of
lacking artistic integrity, of wanting to save his
characters instead of leaving them to be what
they were, of planning his novel as if it were a
sermon and of allowing 'the mildew of evangelicalism' to taint with allegorising didacticism
even his fantasy Tir y Dyneddon. An encouraging
reference (in a supplementary note) to the story
in Y Llenor did little to soften the blow. To a
man of Tegla's hypersensitivity these penetrating
strictures were insupportable and my own

impression is that he resented them all his life. In this taste of 'hell' he even asked T. Gwynn Jones to speak his mind on the subject but nothing came of this (though his friend wrote a general defence of Tegla against his critics in an article in YR EURGRAWN in 1935). Tegla could excuse himself later on for the misery of his despair on the grounds that the blow fell when he was in a state of physical weakness and psychological stress; but he should have taken comfort from Saunders Lewis's accompanying praise of his 'delightful Welsh' and his possession of 'many virtues, fancy, humour and—though fitfully—knowledge of human nature'. He did not afterwards attempt a novel on the scale of GŴR PEN Y BRYN.

But he was by no means crushed. He continued to write for a young audience and in 1927 published two very different works which were greatly praised, IESU O NASARETH (*Jesus of Nazareth*) and HEN FFRINDIAU (*Old Friends*). The former was very different from the conventional portrayal of Christ and was welcomed by those who liked a modern approach as something entirely new in Welsh. HEN FFRINDIAU impressed some as having a more universal originality and although it has been shown by D. Tecwyn Lloyd that one of its main ideas had been anticipated in a piece by Alice Corkran, THE ADVENTURES OF MRS. WISHING-TO-BE, in 1903, it seems most probable that Tegla reached it independently and in any case worked it out in his own way, weaving a network of stories out of hints found in old Welsh nursery rhymes to illustrate the mystery and marvel of being. Tecwyn Lloyd has found in it an 'existentialism' presented a considerable time before the philosophical and literary movement of that name became a main topic of European discussion.

The years 1928–31 were spent at Liverpool where Tegla's central fellowship was at Mynydd Seion chapel, a church which had enjoyed and, like others, flaunted much worldly prosperity but which was now seeing these outward glories fading in a period of deepening depression. Tegla's most notable literary achievement during these years was a series of stories contributed to Y WINLLAN in 1928 and published as a book in 1930 under the title Y DOCTOR BACH (*The Little Doctor*). In these yarns about the lad Robert (the 'doctor') and his friends the country life which the author had known and loved was winsomely re-created. It was well received except for a withering critique by no less a judge than Kate Roberts who declared in an article in Y DDRAIG GOCH that Tegla's art had deteriorated. She added that his attitude to people was marred by a strange interest in ugliness and deformity which he described with crudity before going on to arouse our compassion with some sad incidents affecting the characters thus afflicted. She said too that his method with moral weaknesses was satire and that his best work was purely and directly satirical as in his Pwlpudedig Jones skit; but that in Y DOCTOR BACH he had sometimes put his own sardonic thoughts into the mind of the boy and that in any case his satirical bent had become a kind of complex, the preacher invading the domain of the story-teller and being clever at the expense of his characters. She praised his mastery of Welsh and use of Denbighshire idioms. One wonders whether Tegla was amused by the contrast between Kate Roberts's rebuke of his cruelty towards his characters and the earlier strictures of Saunders Lewis who had said that he lacked 'cruelty or in other terms, artistic integrity', seeking to convert his sinners 'to repentance and amiability'. Of course, the two critics were speaking of different kinds of cruelty and of different books. It is of interest to note that Tegla denounced Saunders Lewis's MONICA in 1931 but cordially praised Kate Roberts's FFAIR GAEAF in 1938. In his Liverpool period Tegla wrote also a further biting satire on the unworthy minister, the kind of man who (in palmier days than the present) had entered the ministry in order to enjoy a comfortable life. This short novel, GYDA'R GLANNAU *(Hugging the Shores)* was written serially for YR EURGRAWN and not published in book form until 1941. Spiritual lethargy among ministers was for Tegla a potent factor in the decline of the churches.

His next sphere of ministry, centred at Bangor, was a particularly happy one, and the extension of a Wesleyan minister's period of service in a circuit from three years to five enabled him to serve there until 1936. In 1931 he published a translation into Welsh of Bunyan's PILGRIM'S PROGRESS—not by any means the first Welsh version of the work but one which was praised by many as the most natural, direct and freshly rendered of them all. In the same year he undertook the editorship of YR EFRYDYDD *(The Student)*, a highly respected periodical of religious and literary interest. For five years he showed great catholicity in his choice of contributors even though he did not seek to wield a powerful editorial pen. The greatest excitement aroused by the journal during this period was the pseudonymous publication of notable poems by T. Gwynn Jones which provoked interest and curiosity. The mischievously sardonic side of Tegla's nature became evident in the comic *pryddest* he submitted to the astonished adjudicators in the Aberafan Eisteddfod of 1932 on the solemn theme, 'He who has suffered has conquered' (Glamorgan's county motto in classic southern Welsh). A much finer achievement is represented by a collection of Tegla's short stories in 1934 under the title Y LLWYBR ARIAN A SAITH STORI ARALL *(The Silver Path and Seven Other Stories)*. It would have been better if he had written more stories of this quality instead of wasting his time and energy in trying to translate E. R. Appleton's AN OUTLINE OF RELIGION FOR CHILDREN into Welsh, a long work scarcely worth the enormous trouble of which he despairingly complains in a letter written in 1934. The growing helplessness of the churches in the thirties brought from him some acid comments in an article in Y CYMRO *(The Welshman)* at the end of the year where he remarks that it would have been odd if Saint Paul had hired a Greek drama group in order to raise funds to clear the Jerusalem church of debt or had organised a dance or a bazaar and asked Herod to perform the opening ceremony. He no doubt found much gratification in the academic and professional successes of his gifted son Arfor at this time.

In 1936 Tegla returned to Manchester where he

stayed until just before the outbreak of the Second World War. While he admired the courage of the Three who burnt the Bombing School soon after his leaving Bangor he showed at this time detachment rather than commitment in his reactions to what was happening in Wales. When Lord Londonderry, a member of the government which had inflicted the Bombing School on Llŷn, was in January 1937 chosen to be one of the presidents of the National Eisteddfod at Machynlleth, five prominent literary adjudicators resigned in protest; and soon afterwards a letter written by Tegla over the pseudonym 'Another Adjudicator' appeared in THE MANCHESTER GUARDIAN, rebuking them for failing to keep their agreement with the Eisteddfod authorities and accusing them of inconsistency over the language issue. On this Huw Ethall shrewdly remarks that Tegla was living in Manchester at the time, a hint that his hero was by no means free from the amphibious nature of the national loyalty of most of the 'good Welshmen' of his period. Perhaps Tegla was finding some difficulty in reconciling a full Welsh patriotism with his Wesleyanism. In his own denomination he was climbing to heights of influence. As President of the Conference at Rhyl he voiced a warning about the dangers threatening the Christian Church from without (world trends in thought and politics) and from within (theological errors), a laboured disquisition which is not among the most inspired of his utterances. He was also invited to deliver the address the following year at Colwyn Bay as part of the celebration of the bicentenary of Wesley's conversion in 1738. This found its way into the pages of YR EURGRAWN and was subsequently published as a pamphlet. Tegla's literary feat at this time (1938) was STORI SAM *(Sam's Story)*, a work which he came to regard as his supreme failure on the grounds that it was praised or blamed for the wrong reasons by critics who had completely missed the point. D. Tecwyn Lloyd sees the story as crowning the whole series of Tegla's books for children and as presenting an experience which transcends ordinary description and imagery and transports us through the dizzy realms of myth into a supramundane condition which nevertheless leaves us unsatisfied and bewildered. The daunting prospect of another hideous war troubled the closing months of his stay at Manchester—with Tegla seeing Hitler as less black than he was being painted and as in any case as being the creation of the powers that were denouncing him.

The war came on 3 September 1939, Tegla having newly arrived to take up pastoral responsibilities at Coed-poeth near Wrexham. The pastoral and the prophetic aspects of the ministry were inevitably soon in conflict within him. It was difficult to give comfort to the families of young men called to the forces and at the same time say that in reality they were not venturing their lives for a good cause but were going out as victims of power politics and the soul-less war machine. He saw the war suddenly solving the unemployment problem of a stricken area and at the same time doing nothing to alleviate the increasing anglicisation of the much loved region where he had spent his youth. There were family anxieties too—the serious illness of his daughter Gwen, the departure of his son Arfor to serve with the

Friends' Ambulance Unit, the constant strain of the war in the home of one who sought to maintain a pacifist witness at a time of increasing hostility to it. There were deaths that affected him, including that of his dearest sister Hannah in 1942 and his old friend Evan Roberts in 1944. In one sense his literary activity became more definitely than ever an aspect of his ministry. He made a selection of passages from the Bible in Y FLODEUGERDD FEIBLAIDD *(The Biblical Anthology)* (1940), and he wrote for YR EURGRAWN a series of dialogues on matters theological and ethical, a work published in volume form after the war, Y SANHEDRIN *(The Sanhedrin)* (1945). In 1943 DECHRAU'R DAITH *(Beginning the Journey)* appeared, written for the guidance of young persons contemplating church membership, and it sold unexpectedly well. Early in the following year a collection of sermons was published, GORCH-FYGU'R BYD *(Conquering the World)*.

His last move in his peregrinations as a Wesleyan minister was to his 'old friends' at Tre-garth in 1944 and there he remained until his retirement in 1946. He undertook a new responsibility towards the end of 1944, the editorship of a new series of handbooks providing information and discussion on a variety of topics, Cyfres Pobun (Everyman's Series). No one doubted either the need for the venture or the quality of its productions, but the series languished for eight years and was then discontinued for lack of public support, a disappointment which led Tegla to say that Welsh literature was facing a life and death crisis. His retirement was perhaps hastened by a grievous decline in his wife's

22

health and was made the easier by the arrange-
ment that they should share the house of their
daughter Dyddgu and her husband, a well known
civic official at Bangor, and by the invitation
extended to him by Meuryn, the editor of the
HERALD CYMRAEG, to contribute a weekly article
to that periodical. He took the pseudonym
'Eisteddwr' (Sitter) which in Welsh Wesleyan
parlance means 'minister in retirement'. It soon
became apparent that a writer of unusual powers
was responsible for Eisteddwr's articles and his
identity came to be generally known. The death
of his wife in May 1948 left him with the sense of
an irreplaceable loss, and something similar must
be said of the death of his friend T. Gwynn Jones
in March 1949. Fortunately Tegla was able to
remain for the rest of his life under the secure
roof-tree of his daughter's home at Bangor.

Collections of Tegla's articles and essays were
inevitable and were well received. RHYFEDD O FYD
(It's a Strange World) (1950) was predominantly
satirical and entertainingly clever. Y FOEL FAEN
(the name of the upland district where his father
had been a quarryman) (1951) and AR DDISBEROD
(Astray) (1954) contained material—of high and
distinctive quality—more in line with his character as an earnest preacher and penetrating
observer. The many who valued his sermons
were glad to have some of them in print in
Y FFORDD (The Way) (1959) and Y DYHEAD (The
Yearning) (1966). His book of autobiographical
sketches, GYDA'R BLYNYDDOEDD (With the Years)
(1952) was welcomed as a classic and was sup-
plemented by GYDA'R HWYR (At Eventide) (1957), a
volume of memories and reflections. His radio

23

talks won increasing acceptance and a selection
of them was published in a slim volume YR HEN
GWPAN CYMUN *(The Old Communion Cup)* in 1961.
His stature was becoming more and more
recognised. The omission of an essay on him in
GWŶR LLÊN *(Men of Letters)*, a collection of studies
of outstanding contemporary Welsh authors
edited by Aneirin Talfan Davies and published
towards the end of 1948, greatly dismayed some
of Tegla's admirers, and one of them, Islwyn
Ffowc Elis, sought to make amends by publishing
a collection of appreciations of his work, EDWARD
TEGLA DAVIES: LLENOR A PHROFFWYD *(Edward Tegla
Davies: Writer and Prophet)*, a volume which appeared
in 1956 and gave him no little satisfaction. Soon
afterwards he found himself in trouble in some
quarters for not showing sufficient respect for
Evan Roberts the revivalist and the severity of
the rebuke which he incurred plunged him into
a condition of confusion which was diagnosed
as nervous tension. But this was a passing episode.
In 1958 he was honoured by the University of
Wales with the degree of D.Litt. and was hand-
somely praised on the occasion by Griffith John
Williams. But he turned down the proffered
honour of an OBE in 1962, feeling, as he wrote
to Dyddgu Owen, that he could not reconcile
acceptance of it with his pledge to serve one who
had perished on a cross. In his last years he had
to face severe operations and he died in hospital
at Bangor on 9 October 1967.

During the years 1946–50 it fell to my lot to
converse with Tegla not infrequently, at meetings, on journeys and in chance encounters on
the streets of Bangor. He was a fine-looking man,

tall, upright, dignified with an admirable head crowned with the kind of white hair that ennobles old age. His hair had formerly been reddish. He spoke excellent Welsh with an engaging Powys flavour, fluently and accurately expressing his lively thought in language that was reasonably pure without being unnatural. There is evidence that his manner could be forbidding to those of whom he could not fully approve and there are some who would trace his occasional interest in the physically misshapen or ill favoured or the mentally subnormal to some kind of limitation of his human sympathy, though the reverse is surely even more true. To those who enjoyed talking with him he gave the impression that he enjoyed talking with them. He was over-sensitive to adverse criticism, partly perhaps because early disadvantages had left him with an understandable but entirely unnecessary sense of the superiority of the academically eminent. I once, rather foolishly, tried to urge him to produce a long epic of fantasy and satire and myth that would make him a peer with Apuleius and Rabelais and Swift, but this was not the best way to thank him for all that he had already done. We can be sure that the sum of that achievement fully merits his inclusion in this series among the 'writers of Wales'.

II

We turn now to Tegla's three well known books
of stories in which the action turns around boys.
HUNANGOFIANT TOMI is written in the winsome
Powys dialect of Welsh or, to be more exact, the
dialect of Llanrhaeadr-ym-Mochnant on the
border between the old counties of Montgomery
and Denbigh. Tomi is an honest and true-hearted
eleven-year-old, and while the author's moral
intent is unconcealed it is for the most part
unobtrusive. The skill of the telling is so assured
that the reader is quickly lured without critical
protest into the little world of Tomi, his ingeniously malicious companion Jac y Foel and
his loyal friend Wil y Llan. Each episode presents
a character or an incident or an aspect of family
or village life—John Williams and his bardic
name; a visit to Tomi's brother, a newly fledged
farm hand still sick for home; the three lads
making themselves ill by smoking; Tomi's
calamitous attempt to give a recitation before an
audience. We see all through Tomi's eyes, and
so the characterisation is of the simplest. Certain
psychological aspects are ignored, but the guile-
less tale engages the sympathies of all but the
most jaded and hardened of readers. Tomi is
voted the best loved of Tegla's characters.

It is not altogether the conventional chapel
morality that Tegla offers. He broadly assures
us that Jesus Christ did not go around asking
every child he saw to recite a verse and Tomi

thinks the cemetery 'a fine place for jumping'. Behind the innocence of Tomi there lurk the gentle wit, broad humour and barbed satire of Tegla in his happiest vein. Tomi takes a rabbit to school, hoping that the teacher will not notice it. The mean and treacherous Jac is jealous:

Jac said, 'I have a plan, Tomi'. 'What's that?' I asked. 'Pull your rabbit out', he said, 'and take hold of its head, and I'll take hold of its tail and pull it a little bit, only a little bit, and if it squeals we shall know that that hurts it, and we'll tell everybody never to do a thing like that to rabbits because it hurts them, but we've got to know first of all whether it does hurt them, you know, before we can say so.' I thought this a rather good plan, that would make us able to defend rabbits in the future, and we got to work on it.

When the teacher hears the rabbit squeal Jac tells him that it belongs to Tomi.

'I'll give you rabbit', said the teacher; but would you believe it? Although he was the teacher he did not keep his word. What he did was to take the rabbit away from me.

Sometimes a *saeva indignatio* smoulders behind the naïve observations of Tomi, as in the account of the well-to-do shopkeeper who refused to give Tomi's grandparents in their dire poverty something to help their sick child at the time of the influenza epidemic. Tomi thinks that the shopkeeper's full name is 'Bot. of Edward Parry':

It was the time when the influenza swooped down on the country and I had to go out in the middle of the night to knock at the shop door and ask for a bit of something. And 'Bot. of Edward Parry' got up to look through the window and ask if

27

*I had the money to pay for it, and when he saw I hadn't he did
nothing but grumble—but after all, perhaps I shouldn't
complain about him too much—he was a first-class man in the
prayer meeting. There was the loveliest tone you ever heard
in his voice when he said in his prayer, 'O Lord, remember
the poor and the needy'.*

In the context this is not badly done: it is better
than Dickens's Pecksniff and much more telling
than anything in Caradoc Evans.

Now and again—let it be conceded—Tegla
attributes to his eleven-year-old sentiments which
would proceed more naturally from an adult
looking back on his childhood, as when he
speaks of the mother's sacrificial devotion to her
home and children in an age of grinding poverty:

*I have heard many people talk about being poor and proud.
Well, all I can say is that I believe that poverty is something
to be proud of if it can make characters who can sacrifice
themselves as Mam did in order to hide it.*

And the death of Tomi's little sister, Lisi Bach,
does not wholly escape from the curse laid upon
fictional treatments of the dying moments of
little girls. Lisi asks to see a primrose. Tomi
gathers some for her and when he comes back
sees deep anxiety in their mother's face and in
the doctor's too.

*I went past them without their knowing and I put a bunch of
primroses in Lisi Bach's hand. She opened her eyes and took
hold of them and smiled at me, and then her head and her hand
fell back, and the primroses fell scattering over the bed; and
every time I shut my eyes in the night, that's the first thing*

28

I see—Lisi Bach smiling with her head on the bed and her eyes closed, and the primroses scattered around her. I have those primroses in a box today—and nobody knows anything about them.

This last bit does not ring true, and perhaps it is all over-simplified and overdone; but there are worse atrocities in Dickens and Harriet Beecher Stowe. Some of us no doubt have reservations about Tomi's grandfather's remarks on old people's memories:

My boy, you can never understand the feelings of an old man and an old woman when the noise of the morning's struggle has changed into music in the distance as evening falls so that they come to feel that it was all music.

One doubts whether an old man who is not an author would express himself in this way, and one doubts even more Tomi's capacity to grasp the words and record them. But despite all such carpings Tomi's story remains a little classic, a precious miniature.

Dyddgu Owen has drawn attention to its value as a picture of Welsh rural life in a by-gone age. Tomi goes around with a knotted kerchief about his neck and ribbed trousers that make a swishing sound as he walks and his elders' clothes are described in like detail. It was the time when a 'cnegwarth o fferins', *a penn'orth of sweets,* was possible and desirable, while a pair of red herrings could be bought for a penny-ha'penny. Following a band and holding a horse's head were moments of pleasurable excitement in a boy's life. All seems effortlessly done. The story's instantaneous acceptance owes much to its being wholly unambitious. Though intended for children and certainly read by some with rapture at the time it succeeded to its author's surprise in being literature for all.

NEDW was arguably an even greater success among children, especially in the hands of a gifted teacher like Dyddgu Owen who could communicate enthusiasm. I suspect that in writing directly about the antics of his boy characters Tegla consciously avoided anything that could savour of Victorian moralism or sentimentality, as do some passages in HUNANGOFIANT TOMI. The ten-year-old Nedw and his cousin Wmffra are pictured as lively, healthy, mischievous lads and in the stories told about them the desire to entertain is given free rein with the minimum of edification. Nevertheless I find the volume less natural as well as less appealing, a bundle of stories without the consistency which makes HUNANGOFIANT TOMI into a short novel or a fragment of one. NEDW falls occasionally into melodrama—as in the fright given by the demented old woman looking for her long-dead child—or into farce—as when the boys paint an old mule to make it look like a zebra—and so loses touch with reality. Caricature tends to supplant portraiture: when Daniel Williams breathes heavily he draws his cheeks in until they meet inside his mouth and when he breathes out his cheeks are blown out like two bladders and between one breath and another he wrinkles his nose and makes it go up and down like a rabbit's. There is an ancient lineage to this kind

of thing in Welsh: we are momentarily trans-
ported into the realm of CULHWCH AND OLWEN.
But it does not help to preserve the verisimilitude
of the book as an evocation of Welsh rural life in
the teens of the century.

NEDW has two characters who are deficient—the
adult Jona'r Teiliwr who is slow-witted and club-
footed and the victim of an elaborate practical
joke and the hopelessly retarded lad Sec who is
helped and protected by the boys. Such characters
exist and the art of fiction should not ignore
them; but it can be argued that Tegla's stories
have a disproportionately high number of them.
This could indicate a concern for the welfare of
nature's unfortunates but it must be said that
Jona at any rate is exploited for comic effect
without a trace of pity or protest. It can, of
course, be argued that the conventions of modern
humanitarianism can be too squeamish and that
a dwarf adopted as a plaything in a royal court
was in olden days to be envied rather than
pitied. On the whole Tegla's fun is good and the
horse kick in Nedw's face seems a fair price to pay
for the ruining of Uncle John's new hat. Of the
stories of mischief and comic incident perhaps
'Bod yn Ddiymhongar' *(Being Modest)* is the best,
the story in which Wmffra's elder brother
William, a College student, visits the homes of
his relatives in order to show that he does not,
despite his acquirement of education, think
himself a cut above them—a display of modesty
which is ill rewarded by the variety of poor
welcomes given him and his younger companions. But the story is rounded off with an
uproarious incident in which a calf instead of

31

behaving like its modest self rushes like a race-horse and comes to a sudden stop like a donkey much to the discomfiture of its rider. Yet it is another story, 'Mafon Duon' *(Blackberries)*, that contains the most delicate example of child observation, the relationship between Nedw and the 'new girl' Jinny Williams, brilliantly captured by the illustrator 'Illingworth' in the best of the drawings he made for the book.

In addition to the stories in which the boys dominate the action there are those in which their role is subordinate. Two of these present remarkable characters—Aunty Laura and Daniel Williams. The story of the former, a hopeless cook, an addicted pianist and a kind soul, is the comic masterpiece of the collection and the story that introduced to Wales the delightful discovery that the famous long place name beginning LLANFAIRPWLLGWYNGYLL could be sung effectively to the well-known yearning hymn-tune 'Tôn-y-botel'. There are also three moving stories in which—indirectly and through the only partial understanding of a child's mind—we are brought into the presence of grief, heartbreak and a sense of outrage in the hearts of adults. The sense of outrage is in the last story in the volume, a story exposing the harsh treatment of the stricken poor by their heartless and rapacious masters; but it is sadly marred by the fact that it is told to the boys by the local blacksmith with a literary compactness and a bitter irony which would have passed over their young heads. The grief in 'Dewyrth a Bodo' *(Uncle and Aunty)* is a tender grief for a child long dead whom Nedw much re-sembles. The heartbreak in 'Gwynt y Dwyrain'

E. TEGLA DAVIES

(East Wind) comes from the news of the death of Nedw's brother Huw in Belgium in the First World War.

There remains what is for me the finest story in the volume, ''Rhen Nedw' *(Old Neddy)*. It is a marvellous attempt to express the inner thoughts and whimsies of a child, Nedw's private world which he cannot communicate fully to anyone else and certainly not to older folk. It seeks to convey especially a child's sense of being im-measurably old, the joy of embracing and kissing an old tree, of communing with the mountain and the stream incarnate as an old couple, of sharing experiences with the old stone heads in front of the mansion of the disgraced baronet who had once lorded it over the neighbourhood. This is an authentic experience of childhood but not fully recognised by children while they are children and not communicable except by a mature artist.

There is much in the writing to attract and satisfy even when the story seems to be uncon-vincing—a sense of detail, a feel for background, a combination of whimsicality and naturalness in the style:

Hannah was writing her name on a piece of bread with what was left at the bottom of a treacle tin, and John was enjoying himself examining gleefully his teeth marks in his bread and dripping.

The new house is a lonely house, at the foot of the Foel, not far from the 'Black Crow'. And on dark nights in the winter there is nothing to be heard but the wind blowing in the

33

oaktrees at the top of the garden and the waterspout near the
pigsty and the sign of the 'Black Crow' screeching when
shaken by the wind.

'Nedw, my boy, wake up', she said. 'You'll lose your chance
to see the dawn breaking, that's certain.'
But I had already for some time reconciled myself to the
prospect of bearing that tribulation without complaint.

Y Doctor Bach makes an entertaining third with
Hunangofiant Tomi and Nedw. Its reception was
mixed. Thomas Parry hinted that it excelled even
the other two; Kate Roberts saw a sad deterio-
ration, finding the children colourless and
deploring the excessive interest in defects of body
and character, and Islwyn Ffowc Elis, while
delighting in its two predecessors has confessed
he is not sure about Y Doctor Bach. 'The Little
Doctor' is a kind nickname given to the boy
Robert by the crazy old woman Martha Edwards
whose pain in her knees is relieved by rubbing
them with a turnip in accordance with the boy's
advice. Other boys in the stories are Robin Slei
and Wil Dau Hanner. 'Y Doctor Bach' is the
story-teller. The stories present curious incidents
or odd characters, not, of course, without an
element of satire. As a boy reared by his grandparents Robert does not appeal to Dyddgu Owen
in the same way as Tomi and Nedw and indeed
she thinks he deserves to be hung up on a
crab-apple tree by his trousers, a fate which
accidentally befalls him in one of the yarns. The
book has value for her as a picture of Welsh
country life and the innocent fun of Welsh
children in a period now for ever lost. Whether

the lost paradise of childhood even in rural Wales was ever as innocent as she supposes is a moot point.

A distinction can, of course, be made between books written about children and books written for children. No doubt these three books were intended to amuse children—boys at any rate—and sometimes to improve them; but, especially in NEDW, there are passages and even whole stories which are beyond the understanding or the sensitivity of a child. Such are stories for adults involving children or mediated through a child's mind. From this point of view I find Y DOCTOR BACH less problematic than the other two volumes, and this is largely because Robert is consciously presented as a particularly thoughtful boy—the real reason, I suggest, why Dyddgu Owen does not like him overmuch. His thoughtfulness in the story 'Bachgen Meddylgar' (A Thoughtful Boy) is shown by his relationship with his grandmother who has suffered a crippling and disfiguring stroke and his asking why, even before the stroke happened, she, who had once been the most attractive young lady of the neighbourhood, had insisted on his sister Sara Elin learning with great thoroughness the text from Proverbs, 'Favour is deceitful, and beauty is vain: but a woman that feareth the Lord, she shall be praised'. Robert is an ethically percipient lad, as when he sees the inconsistency of his parents as they watch the desecration of the Sabbath by a cockfight with their hands over their ears and their eyes wide open. Though he can join with other boys in mischief that is not always considerate he will not allow the humpbacked lad

Ned Grwmp to expose his deformity and at the
end of the story about Ned lets him have the
coveted peacock's feather which gives him in
death a bliss he never knew in life. And in the
last story in the volume, 'Ysglodyn o'r hen
Foncyff' (*A Chip of the old Block*) he is shown to be
a boy who seldom cries but when he does can
hit out at his tormentors in a way worthy of his
grandfather who is well known for having been
able, on the right occasion, to make effective use
of his fists. Tegla had a fighting grandfather. Are
there autobiographical touches here? At the end
of this last story Robert feels an urge to become
a preacher. The volume, though again anecdotal,
is more of an unity than NEDW and gravitates a
little way towards the novel. The young hero
seems to grow by his experiences and his grandparents, though lightly sketched, are real characters.

Two of the stories border on farce. One describes
the *débâcle* that ensues when Hannah Maria,
Robert's eldest sister, brings home her diminutive
but self-important English husband. The other
makes game of a fund-raising chapel bazaar in
which the grand lady who gushingly opens it
topples over onto the floor after leaning on the
nonexistent back of a chapel bench. In both there
is an element of crude satire—on the cheap
arrogance of a certain type of braggart Englishman and on the snobbery and superficiality that
tarnish the efforts of religious fellowships to
remain financially solvent. Each of the two
stories has a kind of moment of truth—when
Robert's grandfather, a warm admirer of the
Englishmen he has known, repudiates the

'sgilffyn Sais' *(the English windbag)* who is his son-in-law and when his grandmother (unlike his mother who becomes a little self-important in her preparations for the chapel bazaar) remarks that it is all over with religion if it has to be bolstered up with shows.

The neatest story—as story—is 'Torri'r Saboth' *(Sabbath-breaking)*, and it is one of the most diverting that Tegla ever wrote. It is clear that the sin of the title is one to be treated lightly in the author's opinion. Wil, the son of Dafydd Williams the carpenter, is an inveterate transgressor. Sunday after Sunday he buys sweets from Betsan Puw's little shop and eats them in chapel. Robert has been warned against this pernicious practice:

Our father always took care to warn us about Betsan Puw's shop, saying that the Bible's advice to us was to pass by on the other side. Whenever he mentioned Betsan Puw's shop he quoted the verse, 'And when he saw him, he passed by on the other side'. And that's what we did—we passed by on the other side as far as we possibly could, until I once went so close to the hedge in passing by on the other side that I tore my best trousers—and then I had it from my mother. This just shows how inconsistent grown-up people are—telling you to pass by on the other side and then when you do so giving you a whacking for it. And I would have been furious with my mother, too, for that whacking, if it were not that there was a blackbird's nest in the hedge exactly opposite old Betsan Puw's house, so that I was killing two birds with one stone as they say by keeping as close as possible to the hedge in order not to go too near old Betsan's house and at the same time taking advantage of the situation to look and see whether there were any eggs in the nest. But of course if I told my mother

37

about this I know she would put the blame on the nest and not on my keeping my father's commandment.

But this is only a part of the appetizer which precedes the meal, the story of the formidable cockerel which vanquishes all comers and brings shame and loss to the Sabbath-breaking tavern-keeper and no little comfort to Robert's naïvely illogical father.

Among those on whom nature has played unkind tricks are Martha Edwards, Olwen Tŷ Tywyrch and of course Ned Grwmp. Despite the fact that in the words of Robert's father Martha is 'a girl who has lost the way' she has a knowledge of the contents of the Welsh Bible, as far as phrases and sentences go, which would put to shame the most scripturally addicted of Welsh preachers. She supports every remark with a Biblical quotation which is as decorative as it is irrelevant; and is a delicious 'flat character' worthy of greater prominence. Olwen Tŷ Tywyrch is the reverse of the Olwen beloved of Culhwch in the famous tale. She is described as thin with mousecoloured hair hanging like candles down her shoulders and past her cheeks, with one lock often straggling over her eyes. Her face has the sootiest hue and looks shiny and wet and is adorned with a turned up nose. She moves with a dragging gait in her patched clothes. She has nothing much to say but turns her eyes to you like a pet lamb hoping for milk. Older than anyone else in the school, she is always at the bottom of the class, spoils every game and will not be shaken off. One day, when she is looking her ugliest, she is rebuked by Robin Slei for letting her side down once

38

again and in her misery she says that she wishes
she were like 'the schoolmaster's sweetheart'
(which is the title of the story, 'Cariad y Scŵl').
'The schoolmaster's sweetheart' is none other
than the Olwen of the old tale, resplendent in
her colours which excel the glorious tints of
nature. The story goes on to describe in doubtful
taste how the boys proceed to try to beautify the
poor girl with the help of grease, flour, red ink
and egg yoke—partly no doubt to mock the
hyperbole of the medieval author of CULHWCH.
But one could not blame a critic for finding in
Tegla's grotesque story something to justify
Kate Roberts's strictures on his unhealthy interest
in the ugly and the repellent. The story about
Ned Grwmp, 'Pluen Wen' *(Peacock's Feather),* may
be regarded as yet another example, but there
Tegla the moralist and sentimentalist takes over,
and Ned relieves the reader by dying in heavenly
joy.

Other stories have extravagant plots which tax
credulity without providing any real compen-
sation in the way of thought or symbolism.
'Gwneud Ewyllys' *(Making a Will)* is the story in
which Robert finds himself suspended by his
trousers over what he believes to be a terrible
cleft in the rock and is teased by his playmates
into making his will leaving his boyish treasures
to his friends. Some of the items show the Little
Doctor's 'thoughtfulness', such as his leaving his
piece of cobbler's wax to Robin whose grandfather
was a cobbler. 'Sêr Awstralia' *(Stars of Australia)*
tells how the boys go down into a deep shaft
with the notion that that could be the way to
reach Australia; and how they see glowing objects

39

which they think must be Australian stars—until
they are disillusioned and humiliated by Bob y
Felin. Some of the accompanying drollery is,
as often with Tegla, better than the plot, like the
idea that people in Australia must be walking
upside down through some device comparable
with whatever enables flies to walk on the ceiling.
In 'Ymarferiad Corfforol' *(Physical Exercise),* about
an attempt to cure a sleepy boy of his lethargy
by taking him on a rowing boat about the lake
in the grounds of the Plas, the mocking style
and extravagance of incident are both overdone;
and this is true also of a story whose initial impact
is delightful, 'Y Dyn Pwysig' *(The Important Man* or
The V.I.P.), which relates the discovery of an
ancient grave in a garden (the grave of a Welsh
chieftain of Roman times whose sitting posture
proclaims his exceptional importance) and goes
on eventually to tell how the boys play war, the
Welsh against the Romans, and how Robert
refuses to fight and is accused of being a traitor
by his fellow-Welsh. I suggest that 'Y Dyn Pwysig'
has no little psychological interest. The Doctor's
refusal to fight is motivated by his 'thoughtful'
desire to keep his red herring (the weapon used
by the Cymry) for his beloved grandmother but
it may reflect Tegla's own discomfort not mainly
as a pacifist perhaps but as one who was politically
lukewarm in the contemporary struggle for
Wales.

As in the other 'children's books' there is no
shortage of passages which enrich the reader's
experience, especially perhaps the reader who has
left his childhood behind. Here are a few samples:

One of the very important things Grandfather can do is spitting. He always aims like an arrow at the same spot at the bottom of the seat in the farthest corner from him. Grandad is always by himself in the pew. Grannie never comes . . . And when Grandad listens he chews tobacco, half lying with his legs along the seat, shrewdly eyeing the preacher from time to time and spitting into the corner at the other end of the pew—so consistently into the same spot that by this time he has made a hole in the floor of the seat in that place. And now Grandad spits straight through it without even touching the sides into somewhere under the chapel.

Grandad chews tobacco steadily through the meeting and every now and again he makes a quiet "whit-too" sound and with the "too" he shoots the spit through his teeth straight into that hole. It's worth while going to chapel when Grandad is there.

The four of us went to see Sam Twlyn after he died. Sam was a boy of my age, a good sort too . . . Grannie told me to be sure to put my hand on his forehead so that I shouldn't get frightened and see him in my sleep afterwards . . . 'You go in', said Robin Slei to Bob. 'You go', said Bob to Wil Dau Hanner. 'You go', said Wil Dau Hanner to me. But not one of us wanted to move. There came more knocking on the door and we heard someone else saying, 'We've come to see Sam'. 'Hurry up, boys,' said Dafydd Williams the Carpenter. 'Come on, Little Doctor', said Martha Edwards gently. And on we went thoughtlessly in order to shut her up. And there was Sam looking more lovely than anyone of us ever thought he could, with something like white, white wool over him and round his head and under his chin. I put my hand on his forehead, and pulled it away as if I had put it on the bar of the grate. And Bob y Felin and Wil and Robin did the same. Above us were Sam's father and Dafydd Williams— Dafydd Williams talking in a low voice and Sam's father swallowing his spittle. And then Dafydd Williams lowering

41

his voice even further and saying to Sam's father in what I thought was something like terror, 'Samuel, have you heard about the bazaar that's to be in the chapel?'

Mam came to Granny's house to see how she was getting on; and as they chatted she remarked that people were saying that the sow had gone through Tomos Huws's shop (a Welsh idiomatic saying meaning that disorder had led to collapse there), *and that they were selling things for next to nothing. 'Why are they selling things cheap because the sow has gone through the shop?', I asked. 'Be quiet', said Mam, 'Little pigs often have their ears too long'.*

I too was very glad to hear that Mr. Edwards (the minister) was likely to call. Bob y Felin and I and the other boys love to hear him talking. He's lost half his voice and tries to do his best with the other half. And so he always talks like the sound of steam pouring out through the spout of a kettle. The poor chap has preached so much, so Grandad says, that he has almost worn his voice out. And since he has a white beard from ear to ear and under his chin and a clean-looking face he looks exactly as if someone has already begun to lay him out before he's dead.

III

There are children also in Iesu o Nasareth,
(*Jesus of Nazareth*), but this gospel according to
Tegla cannot be grouped with the three books
already examined. It is a semi-fictional account of
the life and work of Jesus as seen through the
eyes of a Jewish boy, Ananias. Despite an admirable attempt to achieve accuracy of detail the
little book never comes alive. Dyddgu Owen does
indeed claim that Ananias and his cousin
Abraham are as much 'boys' as Tomi and Nedw.
I am sorry to have to disagree. Those Welsh lads
would never have used the stilted literary
language often put into the mouths of these
first-century Jewish youngsters; and the doings
of Ananias and Abraham seem to be manufac-
tured either to elicit moral admonitions from
the lips of Jesus or to ensure that they are eye-
witnesses of a scarcely credible number of
episodes in his life. They see his baptism and his
temptation and are involved not only in the
Feeding of the Multitude but also in actions taken
by children in the days leading up to the Cruci-
fixion. Lebbaeus, the father of Ananias, is one of
the three Jewish nationalists among the twelve
disciples (with Simon the Zealot and Judas
Iscariot) and wants Jesus to declare himself to be
the Messiah.

Jesus, in this portrait of him, is predominantly a
pacifist seeking some reconciling compromise
between Jewish patriotism and the willingness

43

to co-operate with Roman imperialism, a willingness illustrated in Levi the tollgate official. A
compromise is discernible also in Tegla's presen-
tation of Christ, a compromise between traditional piety and the liberal picture of him
which was in the twenties becoming acceptable
to some of the College-trained ministers, if not to
all in their congregations. The flight of a dove
and the hiss of a serpent accompany, respectively,
the Baptism and the Temptation, but otherwise
there are no external signs of the inner experiences of the Nazarene. On the other hand,
he is credited with an extraordinary gift for
taming wild beasts by his very presence. He is
saddened to hear that Ananias's catapult is used
for shooting at sparrows and teaches the boys that
God loves children, birds and flowers—but does
not mention serpents. The miraculous is not
excluded by any means. We hear not only of the
healing power of Jesus but also of the walking
on the water, the amazing catch of fish and the
increase of the loaves to feed the multitude. On
the other hand, the raising of Lazarus is mentioned as a rumour which may or may not be
believed, and the suicidal stampede of the
Gadarene swine is explained by their fear of the
demoniac (who is neatly identified as the Prodigal
Son). Mary Magdalen is presented as having been
not a woman of loose life but one mentally
unbalanced. Before becoming a follower of Jesus,
we are told, Simon Peter had been much given
to cursing and swearing, and a recurrence of the
old habit gives an additional spice of wickedness
to his denial of Christ. The fact that Tegla is
writing for children accounts partly perhaps for
odd emphases of this kind. His loss of touch in

44

this curious work is evident in two games which he invents for his Jewish children. Instead of Cowboys and Indians they play Jews and Romans and under the influence of Jesus attempt to organise another game, the Kingdom of God, but they fail to get very far with this because all the children want to be God. I consider it most unlikely that any Jewish children would be ready to play the part of Romans and impossible that any Jewish lad would want the role of Jehovah. Tegla's moralism has here bereft him of his judgement.

Later on, in a sermon in GORCHFYGU'R BYD, Tegla was to detach Jesus Christ entirely from earthly movements and ideologies—a way of asserting his ethical glory by endangering his relevance to human concerns.

IV

It is perhaps his gift for evoking a world of fantasy that sets Tegla most definitely apart from other modern Welsh story-tellers, and some of his other 'children's books' owe their existence to this gift to such an extent that they insist on being discussed together.

His TIR Y DYNEDDON (*The Land of Little Men*) bears the sub-title 'Stories about Fairies' but it has no resemblance to any book of traditional fairy tales. It has from the time of its publication in book form been greatly praised and some have seen in it not only a masterpiece of fancy but a mysterious allegory by which elevating truths are conveyed. The elevating truths are certainly there and sometimes the moral is didactically pointed and is open to the charge of being a pulpit platitude, a stricture which need not mean that it lacks profundity. We have seen how Saunders Lewis raised a dissentient voice in the chorus of praise to say that the work was tainted by 'the mildew of evangelicalism'. He called it 'a fairy tale that by its allegorising just misses the conviction of art'. Tegla himself explained that in January 1917 the waterfall known as Pistyll Rhaeadr, traditionally reckoned as one of the Seven Wonders of Wales, was frozen and re-mained so for a month presenting a glorious spectacle that attracted visitors, and that after seeing it on 29 January he began to write his stories. He added that the description of the

Temple of Ice was not the product of his imagination but a photographically factual picture of
the frozen waterfall which he had visited a
number of times to ensure accuracy. He further
remarked that the deep thoughts some reviewers
had seen in the work had not been intended by
him: all that he had done was to try to conjecture
what creatures could have made such a temple
the centre of their life. This disclaimer must have
been made, partly at any rate, in order to counter
the charge of homiletic didacticism. If Saunders
Lewis condemned, others praised, but the nature
and fervour of their commendation may suggest
that they were sufficiently 'Victorian' in their
tastes to welcome a little sermonising in literature. Thus Ifor Williams, lauding a friend, spoke
of the work's 'tender evangel' and its promul-
gation of 'the divine laws implicit in the spiritual
life of humanity', while Idris Bell solemnly
extolled 'its profound philosophy'.

Of course, a work of art can sometimes proclaim
a truth which the artist did not consciously
intend to teach. Its meaning may be wholly or
partly beyond the immediate awareness of its
creator. John Gwilym Jones and the late Hugh
Bevan are, I would say, among the Welsh critics
who have detected in certain literary works
implications not fully contemplated by their
authors. It may be that some have seen meanings
in TIR Y DYNEDDON of which Tegla was unaware
or only dimly aware; but he must have been
conscious of some, such as that in the sentence
which Parry Williams—no Victorian he—regarded as unworthy in that it openly conveyed
a moral: 'So all the singing of the creation is joy

founded upon sacrifice'. The preacher is clearly at work here marring the achievement of the artist.

It is in the earliest section of the book that love and sacrifice are enthroned. The boy who tells the tale has fallen into a cleft in a rock in his garden and finds himself in a new world, a world in which the growing of the grass is audible and his own voice louder than thunder and the crawling of flies like the trotting of horses. He sees little men about an inch in height, shaped like the letters of the alphabet. They think that the boy's body is a huge mountain. The boy becomes aware that the very life of the Little Men is derived from him. He has an eye which is their sun. When he closes it they are in darkness; when he opens it he bestows sunlight upon them. It is to him that they pray. It seems clear that the boy-mountain is virtually their God. There may also be another quite different range of reference. The boy who tells the tale is an image of the author and the animated letters of the alphabet are the creatures of the literary imagination.

The Little Men pray to the boy-mountain to choose a king for them. The 'dynan' (little man) destined for kingship is the winsome letter N (En), pale and passionate, and he proves his worth by climbing the boy-mountain in order to hear his voice and receive his revelation. The climb is difficult and dangerous, and the climber when he reaches at last the boy-mountain's shoulders is bruised and bleeding; but he struggles up to the face and beholds the glorious sun

48

which is the eye and hears the voice telling him that the toil and the agony of the climb are necessary in order that the ultimate secrets may be revealed. En is hailed as king when he returns to his fellows and a lovely girl, acting solely on an impulse of compassion, washes his blood and tends his wounds. The Little Men join in an act of worship to the boy-mountain, the service including reading from a scroll, dancing and singing—and the offering of a mouse as a sacrifice—an unfortunate incongruity which I find inexplicable unless we suppose that the satirist in Tegla refused at this point to be repressed. Later our narrator hears the ringing of bells, and his own tears turn to song and take the shapes of angels and saints. He realises that in the Land of the Little Men it is from tears that temples are made. He now sees a marvellous procession full of lovely sound and colour as the world of nature honours the king and queen whose marriage is now to be solemnized, the marriage of *En* with *Eg* (the letter G), the beautiful maiden, adorned with rings and gems, who brought him care and healing. Their names are fused together to make *Eng,* the magic sound that underlies all the myriad cadences of the universe. It is in this context that Tegla says that 'all the singing of the creation is joy founded upon sacrifice'. Whether the prominence of the *ng* sound in Welsh, often seen at the beginning of a word as the result of the mutation of an initial *g* under the influence of a preceding *n*—a phenomenon which an occasional English philistine takes it upon himself to mock—has anything to do with this odd piece of Teglaesque ingenuity I do not know; but it seems not unlikely.

Life is brief in Tir y Dyneddon and the happiest
are the children. Some of these like *Ec* (C) and
Ii (I) are full of mischief but they are judged by
their intentions and not by their deeds. In what
promises to turn out to be a sort of Utopia or
Paradise children are not punished for the
curiosity which prompts them to pluck unripe
fruit or to experiment in ways which end up in
some unexpected calamity. In any case nobody
is hurt as they play in this enchanted land: they
fall unscathed off a vanishing rainbow or from
the retracted rays of the stars. But the admonish-
ing preacher cannot help chiming in to say that
too much play can lead to dust and dimness and
an indifference to everything except playthings—
and 'that is the reason why life is not all play in
the Land of the Little Men'. But play in due
proportion and in accordance with the King's
will is good as *Ec* and *Ii* and their companions
discover. Seeking to emulate their King these
merry young fellows climb the boy-mountain;
but drinking of his tears awakens in them two
conflicting longings—for things hitherto un-
imagined and for home and father and mother.
The latter desire prevails and they hasten down.
Their hurrying changes into a merry game of
playing wheelbarrows which gives rise to a
proverb, 'Who would be joyous let him be a
wheelbarrow'. The King, who himself takes part
in the game, points out that the way to learn to
make a wheelbarrow is by acting as the wheel of
a barrow oneself, as indeed *Ec* (shaped appro-
priately as the letter C) has done. Bearing burdens
is thus the sure way to bliss. Soon the children
are able to devise a carriage on the same principle.
Some want to make *Ec* king because of the

50

usefulness of his inventions, and the King willingly agrees, but *Ec* insists that a more precious gift than that of the inventor is the gift of hearing the messages of the mountain and the stars and the clouds—by which Tegla, refraining this time from pointing the moral in so many words, seems to proclaim the superiority of spiritual experience to material progress.

The next episode is the dying of the flowers and the misery of the Little Men in their desolation. Their realm is not a paradise of immortality. *Aa* and *Em,* considered to be rash and foolish, venture into the Dark Land behind the boy-mountain to find the abode of the wizard who knows the secrets of the flowers, and he tells them to seek the two Hidden Roses who are the parents of all the flowers of the world and who dwell in the uttermost snows. They undertake the long bleak journey but *Em*'s strength fails and despite all *Aa*'s devoted care he dies at last— but in joy and on a bed of flowers, the Hidden Roses he sees as he looks up into *Aa*'s face. *Aa* struggles back to Tir y Dyneddon and finds the land in bloom; but he is accused of having killed *Em* and sets out to the Dark Land pursued by his baleful enemies. Crossing over into the Dark Land he reaches the Great Silence where his bitter sorrow overwhelms him and his tears make a pool in the snow. In the reflection of his face in the pool he sees the Hidden Roses glowing in his cheeks and falls into the sleep from which there is no awakening. It seems that Tegla is here abandoning the notion of the Land of Little Men as an utopia in which goodness is enthroned and children are blest and secure. We see it now as under the curse of death and as a world in which the devoted and the adventurous are maligned and persecuted. On the other hand, we are led to see that in the rhythm of nature winter yields to spring and that beyond this world there is a realm in which suffering is transmuted into beauty.

In the story which follows it becomes even more evident that the Land of Little Men is by no means as harmonious as we had been led to hope. The lonely and despised hero is the forlorn *Di* (the letter D) who is something of an outcast because he does not belong to either of the two great clans among the Little Men, the clan to which *Aa, El* and *Aitsh* belong (A, L and H, letters made of straight lines, though Tegla does not deign to explain this) and the clan to which *Ec* and *Oo* belong (C and O, curving letters). *Di* (D) is a mixed-up kid teased and tormented by the rest. One day after being plagued in this way he falls to weeping and one tear falls on the back of his hand. He sees in it a tiny little creature like himself—his reflection, though Tegla leaves us to guess this and much else. *Di* feels that the tiny fellow is gentle and friendly, but the tear grows less and disappears. Afterwards *Di* finds friendly faces looking back at him from the morning dewdrops. This brings him joy but one of the other Little Men discovers his secret and *Di*'s cry of anguish causes the grass to tremble and shed its dew and so his friends vanish away. Thereafter the grass trembles out of sympathy with poor *Di* and so there are no more dewdrops in his world. But afterwards *Di* finds new friends in the raindrops hanging from the gorse blossoms until a malign fellow-*dynan* sees him looking into a bush and shakes it so that the raindrops fall. After that the bushes are shaken every morning by his enemies and *Di* finds himself again in a friendless world. One evening he hears hidden music proceeding from the cascade of tears that flows behind the ice of the Temple and the song awakens some new sensation within him. Moving towards the Temple he sees mirrored in the ice a splendid person looking with longing upon him, a marvellous friend whose companionship he thenceforth seeks day by day. He himself grows in beauty and strength as he daily communes with his gracious friend. The persecution is renewed and the jealous *dyneddon* smash the ice. But the image in the ice becomes united with *Di* himself and in time the inhabitants of the Land come to know that the one who is *Di*'s friend can never be slain. The friend is clearly an image of Christ who is both a reflection of our humanity in search of love and a manifestation of the everlasting love that seeks and saves the lost. But the Land of the Little Men is here a fallen world in which the innocent and the tender are hunted relentlessly by envy and cruelty.

The final chapter tells us of the Little Harpist. The generations pass by, the climate changes and the Temple gradually dissolves. At last the Little Harpist appears and his music entrances all. The more they listen the more lovely and compelling it becomes. When asked the secret of his song the harpist shows that all his music is culled from the hidden sounds of nature—the movement of the waters, the growth of the flowers, the laughter of children, the toil of men.

His hearers begin to dance, their hearts full of love, the one for the other, and this enriches the harp with a new chord.

Partaking of this final joy the boy who is the mountain comes to himself in his own home. His mother is tending him after the accident in the garden, washing one eye and removing from the other a piece of ice which she has put there to prevent him from having a black eye. He remembers how playing with his brother and sister he fell into the cleft of the rock.

The book lacks cohesion, the nature of this strange and beautiful other world varying with the particular 'truths' to be conveyed in its episodes. As in many of Tegla's books the interest flags in consequence of the weakness of his architectonic sense. For some the moralizing and evangelising overtones are tiresome even when they are obscure. Others might find some of the ingenuities a little quaint. But the work certainly has real beauty and originality. It owes much not only to the impact of the frozen waterfall but also, as a foreword tells us, to our ancient habit of personifying mountains (speaking of the foot and the breast and, more often in Welsh than in English, the head) and the delight of some children, especially when taught in a particular way, in humanising the letters of the alphabet. The finest sections are the early one about the king and the queen and the tale of the finding of the Hidden Roses. There are passages like these:

The ice took every form that could be imagined, some of them never yet conceived. On the left it became a band of angels about to close their wings as they descended to the earth. These half open wings were like splendid canopies richly and delicately hemmed. Towards the middle my tears took the form of saints with their hands hiding their faces in prayer. Over the immensities above them there stretched gorgeous curtains and under their feet were mounds of marble and at their sides pillars like the pillars of a temple, and there was radiance everywhere. All around were colours, green and yellow and white. Under the ice there flowed the tear drops that had not been frozen, all of them resounding as if there were a great bell awakening all the land.

They could scarcely see him when they came there, so white was he. His garments were spun out of snowflakes, he wore a snow mantle, his face shone with a snowy light, snow were the fringes of his hair and beard and his speech was like the roar of a snow shower driven by the wind.

RHYS LLWYD Y LLEUAD *(Grey Rhys of the Moon)* does not pretend to a like 'profundity'. This story of a visit to the moon by two boys, of twelve and thirteen years of age, Richard (Dic y Nicol) and Moses (Moi'r Mul Du), is a compound of fantasy and fact. I know of one schoolmaster who used it to illustrate the conditions that obtain on our much contemplated satellite. I suspect that he must have been one of very few, if not indeed unique. The combination of the fantastic and the factual unfits the little work for that purpose, and even when he wrote it Tegla was too venturesome in some of his assumptions. Children who enjoy the fairy tale element in the story may find the scientific explanations something of a bore, while those who like straight-

55

forward information are likely to show little respect for Rhys Llwyd and his brother, Shonto'r Coed, King of the Fairies.

The two boys are simply differentiated, Dic being the jollier and the more adventurous and Moses the softer and the tenderer. Both are not enamoured of the religious meeting called the 'seiat' and of having to recite Bible verses—matters on which Tegla's frank lenience cannot have helped parents to maintain a firm discipline. At the beginning of the story they are lurking in a sand hole instead of hastening to the seiat. Rhys Llwyd, the Man in the Moon, comes down and speaks to them, a tiny old man with a stoop and a thin body and a pinched face—and, in W. Mitford Davies's illustrations of him, a big nose and huge ears and long legs. He invites the boys to go with him to the moon, but they have to eat moon apples to provide them with breath, for the moon is airless. Through Moses' tears the colours of the rainbow are to be seen in heavenly beauty, and knowing Tegla we suspect a moral here. Landing on the desert of the moon they find they cannot hear their voices and have to lip-read. Noiselessly rocks fall and make craters. The boys find that they can jump up to about twelve yards off the ground. They see the earth, reminding Dic of maps in the geography books. For Rhys Llwyd the earth is the abode of his brother Shonto and the fairies. Shonto succeeds in reaching the moon on a ray of light. We are told what a person on the moon would experience when people on earth see an eclipse of the moon, and Tegla cannot resist pointing the moral by making Shonto remark that things go wrong when something stands between us and the light. It turns out that Rhys is an exile from the earth, a fairy prince blasted to the moon by the sudden release of a vast deal of air from the body of a fairy windbag called the Llotyn Mawr; but sometimes when that symbol of evil is in a drunken stupor after imbibing an excess of wind it is possible for Rhys to return to earth by sliding down on a moonray. The boys have longings to return to the earth but their passage is more complicated. When their moon apples lose their effect they melt and become two lakes and afterwards two clouds which after passing through the Great Whirlpool between the earth and its satellite become two earthclouds and then two lakes on the earth's surface before being reconstituted with the help of Shonto and his tribe as the two boys they are. Rhys Llwyd's exile too is ended, for his enemy has exploded into little bits which are, however, liable to poison human beings. The story has some ingenuities and a few sententious touches which must be omitted in a bald summary. Dyddgu Owen and Tecwyn Lloyd both praise the work as eminently successful in that it presents a fantastic world in which a child's imagination feels delightedly at home; but I do not recollect, as I do in the case of HUNANGOFIANT TOMI, any confirmation from someone who first read it as a child. On the other hand, it has a quaint originality and a dreamlike fancy which set it apart from most modern fairy stories.

Tegla's virtues, of course, are constant in all he wrote—a clean style, an inventive imagination, a sense of the moral relevance of art, even though this last can become too obvious. Perhaps he was teasing himself when he wrote these words as he described the condition of the boys after changing into clouds:

They did not answer him a word. A cloud cannot speak except when it thunders. Thunder is the voice of the cloud. And they were too young to have learnt to thunder. When clouds grow old and heavy they learn to thunder. And according to Shonto of the Woods it is not very different among human beings. That is his weakness—he keeps on and on giving advice and pointing morals—another sign of old age.

At the age of forty-five Tegla was as addicted to this as Shonto.

As a fantasy HEN FFRINDIAU is the most consistent and successful that Tegla wrote. Its 'existentialism' is for our amusement and belongs to a different world from that of the Existentialist movement that followed the Second World War. The Old Friends of the title are characters briefly pictured in old Welsh nursery rhymes, like the Red Cobbler of Rhuddlan and Dafydd with his New Shoes. Their roles are fixed by the makers of the verses which have given them existence and, strive as they may, they cannot escape their destinies. Even mingling their fortunes does not ultimately deliver them.

Tegla does the mingling ingeniously. The Red Cobbler, failing, as is his fate, to drown the cat, is pushed into the river by the Horned Sheep grazing on the shore. He rides the silver-shod Yellow Foal all the way to the White Barn, the destination appointed in the traditional verse. He makes the acquaintance of the Hen that Lays an Egg a Day and the Cock that Lays Two (according to a fated pattern entertainingly explained) and afterwards encounters the Soldier who in keeping with the rhyme sets his dog on the Horned Sheep. He and the Soldier see the Woman on the Tree-top whose very being is involved in her crying out 'Hooroo, hooroo, hooroo' because she has a hot potato in her throat. She is by no means grateful for the Cobbler's kindness in pulling the potato out, for the act deprives her of her livelihood sealed to her in the verse which gives her being.

'What has the verse to do with our livelihood?' he asked.
'Well, this is the daftest man I've ever seen', said the woman. 'The man who made the verse fashioned my life, didn't he? Because I didn't exist before he made the verse.'
'Yes', said the Red Cobbler with a half sigh. 'But what's the use of it all?'
The woman raised her hands in horror and turned her eyes up so that only the whites were to be seen. 'Don't ask questions, not on your life', she said, with dread in her voice. 'Don't ask questions. My business is to obey. The man himself, the man who made the verse, knows why.'

The woman, however, is (perhaps inconsistently) not extinct, and is very ready to go off arm in arm with the red-coated Soldier. On comes John of the Summer Cot—Siôn y Foty in the old rhyme— and is disappointed to lose the Tree-top Woman, giving vent to his misery in smiles and laughter rather than sighing and weeping.

Next we meet Dafydd of the New Shoes (purchased, inevitably, from the Cobbler). He is the son of the Mother at the White Rock and is happy in the lot appointed to him—wearing his new shoes and keeping his old ones for the summer. Others are by no means contented— John, for example, and the Red Cobbler himself and Will of the Wall, the boy whose fate is to say 'Well' to every wall and never to receive an answer. Eventually—after much interesting virtuosity of wit and logic—we find Dafydd in a state of perplexity and frustration. Summer has come, and he should be wearing his old shoes. When he does so he loses the respect of the Fair Yellow-headed Girl. To win her love he resumes his new shoes and his confusion returns. He even begins to talk backwards. He is driven to plan Revolution.

Like many other revolutionaries Dafydd finds it difficult to acquire dependable fellow-conspirators and difficult even to identify the oppressor. Meeting Little Ifan, fated always to find sea-water cold, he seeks to warm the sea. On their way to do so they help themselves to two horses whose owner is fast asleep in his cart. He is Siôn Huws, the anti-hero of that masterpiece of folk verse which tells us that when he awoke he was not sure who he was but knew that if he were Siôn he had lost his horses, while if he were not Siôn he had somehow become the possessor of a cart.

Dafydd and Ifan come to see that if they are to be free their revolution must be directed against the makers of the verses. In practice all they can do is to write their own verses on paper and destroy them, even though this would, they feel, mean depriving themselves of existence. They burn the papers but find themselves still very much alive—and indeed immortal. Then they see under the moon children playing and girls dancing—the theme of an artless little traditional verse of no little charm. And they are singing the verses in which all the characters of the story exist. The children have been taught them by their mothers; and since this is so, as Ifan remarks, the odd little people will not suffer wrong. With this touch of perhaps too homely sentiment a remarkable work of art and of parabolic thought richer than a brief summary can convey comes to its end.

STORI SAM *(Sam's Story)*, has proved to be the most problematic of Tegla's fantasies. Some readers called it an allegory and found the allegory either tiresome or, even if puzzling, probably profound. Some reviewers, knowing Tegla of old, felt that the theme must be that of a young soul glimpsing the glory of the 'vision splendid' and lavished praise on the work without having properly read it. Tegla, seeing his book so grossly misunderstood, pronounced it his 'greatest failure' and provided his own explanation of his intention. The story was meant to be a study of escapism. The fantasies are Sam's own daydreams, the escapist imaginings of a country lad before he settles down like his parents to accept his unromantic inferiority and to seek to rival the enviable townsfolk only in the art of making money. And so the frustrated adolescent talks of the wondrous things he has seen among the mountains. First, he tells of the Storm Dog who

gathers his sheep together before the storm, the sheep that look like huge bales of wool drifting past the mountain slopes. Of this, and of the one wild sheep of which he must beware, he has heard from his father. When Sam goes to school he adds further tales in order to impress the town boys. He tells of putting his hand into the Cold Brook Spring and grasping a stone at the bottom and in consequence hearing the sound of a bell and seeing an ancient church and the Old Man of the Spring showing him the Storm Dog's Wild Sheep like a cloud speeding past the hill towards the distant mountains. The sight of the Sheep gives him strength and vigour and swiftness and enables him even to spring out of a treacherous bog. We are to understand that this is Sam's compensatory boasting. When he reaches court-ing age he finds himself once again outclassed by the town youths, and so we have the fantasy in which he sees a girl of his own age and hears her crying out to him, 'Boy of the World, come after me'. He hastens after her and flies into the air to follow her; but whenever he tries to grasp her she eludes him and speeds farther on. They come to an immense cave with leafless trees growing in it and the girl explains that they are hairs in a cloud's nostril and when he shakes one warns him of the terrible danger of making the cloud sneeze. This is one of the places where a kind of surrealist humour peeps out in Tegla's narrative. It turns out that all the life of the earth is but the product of the cloud's mind—lovely thoughts like spring and summer and dark thoughts like winter. The girl, who tells him all this, is also one of the cloud's thoughts. Their situation becomes confused—as does a reader's attempt to provide a coherent interpretation of all this—when a battle is fought between their cloud and a black cloud who is his enemy. We are also told that in cloud warfare neither side wins, that the warring clouds melt together and that the sun is the conqueror of all the clouds.

The girl's beauty is described as reflecting the hues of the sun and the sky and a passing red cloud—

Her hair was like pure gold, and her eyes like the blue of the sea when there is a light cloud between it and the sun as it reaches its zenith on a summer's day, and her cheeks were like blood—

and as they journey in a little cloud ship and have little adventures she assumes a supernatural glory. She plays heavenly music with her hands on the rays of the stars and is pleased to see that Sam hears it; but when, watching the dawn, she perceives that Sam is not stirred by it as she is, she speeds away, and he becomes one of many boys and girls who are seeking her. At the end of the story we see Sam compounding his losses by making money through selling eggs.

Tegla's reviewers may, I think, be pardoned for not grasping his intention. In the fantasy about the girl he allows his imagination an excess of free play in directions grotesque and parabolic and loses touch with the psychology of adolescence. Yet the work has been greatly praised by D. Tecwyn Lloyd who says that Tegla's art, as employed in his children's books, here reaches its utmost perfection in a story which transcends itself in a realm of myth comparable with that of the Mabinogi and the Romances. That Tegla had a great gift of myth-making I would not deny but I think it better employed in TIR Y DYNEDDON in one way and in HEN FFRINDIAU in another.

V

One of Tegla's most ambitious works was the novel Gŵr Pen y Bryn. It tells the story of a spiritual development or conversion against the background of the so-called Tithe War of the 1880s and has its real value as a historical novel. Unfortunately its didactic purpose was made too obvious by the sub-title with which it was originally published and which proclaimed that its theme was 'the Awakening of an Ordinary Soul', and by its three divisions which indicated that the sluggish soul was challenged by a voice within himself, by the voice of the country and by the voice of God. It was too much like a sermon, as Saunders Lewis pointed out. On the other hand there is no artistic law against making conversion the theme of a novel so long as the work is done convincingly, and the author should not be accused of softness towards his characters unless his handling of them is clearly sentimental. Tegla, as we have seen, is not entirely free from sentimentality and at times somewhat prone to sententiousness; but this should not blind us to the virtues of a novel which after all is no more 'didactic' in intent than those of Dostoyevsky or Tolstoy. Its principal fault is over-compression. If Tegla could have allowed himself as much canvas as the Russian novelists his achievement might very easily have been comparable with theirs. One reviewer indeed in 1954 rashly classed the novel with the masterpieces of Dostoyevsky, Cervantes and Kafka. But no: it is far too shortwinded, like many Welsh novels (mainly for economic reasons), and so it frequently tells us that a character is pure or gentle or weak or cunning instead of letting the character show us as much in word and deed—or their omission. It has been translated into English by Nina Watkins and published under the title THE MASTER OF PEN Y BRYN. It must be reckoned as one of Tegla's failures, despite a promising plot, an interesting background and episodes that deserved to come off.

The Master—though the Welsh word 'gŵr' does not sound as upper-class as the English word 'master'—is John Williams, a weak and easily tempted man who in his youth has been disappointed in some of his hopes and has followed his father as farmer. He is in comfortable circumstances, but this is due more to his father's than to his own exertions; and now in middle age he is thinking of retiring from his labours. We are told something of the indiscipline of his younger days—his share in the degradation of Mali Ffransis and his having to get married to Jane Roberts and in consequence to give up his plan to enter the ministry. He is aware that he does not enjoy the respect of the community—an agricultural community in northern Powys or southern Clwyd—and dreams of doing something heroic to win his neighbours' admiration. His opportunity comes when he hears the minister T. Cefnllech Roberts say that Wales is awakening and that some courageous farmers are defying the tyranny represented by the tithe. He decides somewhat nervously to join them and urged by his wife he asks the minister to help him to be chosen to preside at a concert at which he can make a rousing speech. Soon the name of Pen y Bryn takes its place in the roll of honour among the anti-tithe campaigners when the auctioneers arrive and encounter local defiance. The speech at the concert raises John Williams to the height of popularity. But soon afterwards to his consternation he unexpectedly receives notice to quit his farm and to avoid the disaster follows his wife's advice and secretly makes abject submission to the bishop. Soon comes another misfortune. Two sheepdogs in the district have turned killers. One of them is killed by John Williams's dog Rofar, and Rofar like his master becomes a hero. Then John Williams discovers that his Rofar too is a killer. Filled with horror and pity he decides to conceal his dog's guilt. His secrets are known to Dafydd Huws the carpenter, but it is not craven fear that makes him confess his weakness to the world but the courageous and trusting death of the devout and gentle old peasant Mathew Tomos. He is converted and acknowledges 'the Love that can love only the holy and the pure and the exalted'. He makes public confession of his deceitfulness and coward- ice. His story ends with a peaceful death and Rofar, now old and blind, finding a new friend in Dafydd Huws. It must be said that some of the later passages in the novel would be more appro- priate in a book of sermons.

Dafydd Huws himself experiences something like a conversion. At first he is scheming to hasten John Williams's retirement in the hope that his own near relatives may take possession of Pen y Bryn. Knowing Williams's guilty secrets he is able to bring pressure to bear upon him. But he himself is a disillusioned and embittered idealist and for him the symbol of purity and love is an innocent and tender maiden. In his youth he saw this symbol embodied in Jane Roberts but she deeply disappointed him and married John Williams. It is the rediscovery of the symbol, this time truly embodied in Annie, daughter of Jane and John, that saves him. The combination of crafty worldliness and a romantic idealisation of maidenly purity needs to be presented with careful and painstaking detail to be made convincing, and Tegla has not done that for us. Another study of disillusionment is the character of the Reverend T. Cefnllech Roberts. We cannot call it a cruel self-portrait of the author, but there can be no doubt that this thumbnail sketch of ministerial frustration and weakness draws on Tegla's own experiences. Early in his ministry Cefnllech Roberts protested against licentious behaviour accompanying the holding of a fair in his neighbourhood but found little support— Tegla's own experience at Porthaethwy. Since then Cefnllech Roberts has come to see for himself that ministers are so ill-paid that they have to accept gifts of farm produce from rich members of their flocks and so quickly lose their capacity for leadership. He can talk glibly and ineffectually about Wales awakening but fails to do anything positive—or to stand by John Williams at the time of his public confession. Yet he too has a sort of spiritual renewal and says that John Williams has restored his visions.

D. Tecwyn Lloyd, for whom GŴR PEN Y BRYN is a great novel, points out the symbolic signifi-

cance of much of the accompanying material.
There is, for example, the half-wit Huw Pant yr
Afon who thinks he is two persons, Huw and
Huwcyn, and who reflects the conflict between
the two sides of John Williams's personality.
There is the daisy trampled underfoot, an image
of the degradation of Mali Ffransis. There is Rofar
the dog who like his master wins a false glory.
There is the use made of the old song 'Y Deryn
Pur' as a symbol of chastity and beauty. And
there is the affinity in contrast between the types
of innocence that help to change the lives of
Dafydd Huws and John Williams and perhaps of
Cefnllech Roberts, too—the innocence of young
love and the innocence of a trusting old man
dying after a life of hardship and subjection and
the innocence of penitence. That we have here—
especially when we consider also the value of the
work as a picture of rural life in Tegla's native
region a hundred years ago—the raw material of
a great novel I make no doubt, but have to record
that Tegla has not given us a work that could be
so described. Gilbert Ruddock in his most
appreciative analysis of the plot remarks how
tidy it all is, but cannot refrain from adding that
perhaps it is too tidy.

Some illustrations by Illingworth added to the
attraction of the volume when it was first published, and the picture of Mathew Tomos and his
family before the fire in their humble home,
reproducing some features of the hearth that
Tegla himself remembered, made a lasting
impression upon me when I first read the novel.
The flavour of the style—or rather styles—of the
book also lingers. In many passages Tegla is

clearly a conscious stylist. At the beginning the writing has a touch of comic irony as when Shôn Bach, one of John Williams's farm hands, makes innocent fun of the contrast between his tall, thin master and the egg-shaped Dafydd Huws as he follows them in a protective capacity at night:

Shôn's way of picturing them was to raise the forefinger of his left hand and the closed fist of his right hand. The Master of Pen y Bryn was the one and Dafydd Huws the 0 . . . After that night everybody knew who were meant when mention was made of Number Ten.

At other times Tegla resorts to elaborate simile as in a paragraph which begins like this:

Like the incoming tide of the sea the excitement of the tithe war came to Llangeunant and the surrounding countryside. At the beginning it was a kind of strange rumbling in the distance that people did not understand—a subject for jocularity and anxiety and boast and foreboding. Then a wave came . . .

He uses the sea in a different way to introduce a phase in John Williams's personal fortunes:

There are some lovely intervals on a summer day when the sea seems to have a stillness, a complete stillness, without even a single wave moving on it or the merest swell on its surface. And a half-dreaming visitor on its shore may suppose that its constant, ceaseless motion has for ever come to an end and that at last it is allowed to rest from the incessant upward pull to which it is subject; and that the moon too, despairing of winning it to her, has allowed it to sink into the quietude it desires. And to behold this is for the visitor, who knows of its tempestuous moods and its calamities, a comfort—to behold the sea, of all things, become still. But as he continues to gaze thus, a little wave is discerned rising in the distance, a wave which, so magical is the tranquillity, is not expected but which when it comes utterly destroys the evenness of the sea. And so it resumes its restless, constant, unceasing movement in response to the summons from above.

For all I know this kind of writing may have an honoured lineage going back to the ancient epic simile. Here it is an inorganic embellishment. Not so the metaphor of the river in John Williams's speech of confession:

We are taught every day that we are people on a journey, as the river is on its journey to the sea . . . And although it's on its journey there are times of cold when we see it taking hold of the earth. So it is with us . . .

But these words had been originally written—in Welsh, of course—not by Tegla but by his patient and humble father, only semi-literate and cruelly disfigured after an accident at work many years before.

His short novel GYDA'R GLANNAU is much less ambitious and, I would say, much more successful. It is a neat example of Tegla's gift as a satirist. It is by Tegla's own testimony the 'story of an artful minister who entered the ministry for what he could get out of it rather than for what he could put into it'. Tegla afterwards regretted having published it, feeling that the calamitous decline in the strength of the churches and their ministries was a more than sufficient judgement

71

on the unworthy ministers who had come under
his lash. In manner it is a skit rather than a
serious novel, mocking not only the worst
specimens of ministers but also the traditional
type of ministerial biography.

Tegla's hero, the eminent Reverend William
Cicero-Williams, began life without any 'Cicero'
in his name. He displayed an early aptitude for
memorising verses of the Bible especially for
financial reward. He felt his divine 'call' to the
ministry when he saw the luscious chicken dinner
prepared for a visiting preacher. He went to great
trouble to choose an impressive ministerial name
for himself but apart from that always chose the
easiest and safest way, 'hugging the shore', as the
title says. 'Hypocrisy' seems to be too serious a
word to describe the professional superficiality
and insincerity of this caricature of the worldly
pulpiteer. It is not suggested that all ministers
are like him, for he is briefly contrasted with a
different kind of minister, one so dedicated to
his calling that, as is sometimes said, 'he burns
himself out'. Has Tegla in this most entertaining
work perpetrated the ultimate in prophetic
cynicism by presenting a sinner not worth saving?
The conclusion has puzzled the critics. Some
have felt that it describes a sort of conversion—
without, apparently, the author's good grace.
Tegla himself said that he had not provided this
sinner with a genuine conversion. It may be that,
with a wary eye on his critics, he decided to avoid
that tricky task; but it is more probable that he
felt that the salvation of Cicero-Williams was
beyond his earthly maker.

72

VI

The more literary of Tegla's short stories are collected in Y LLWYBR ARIAN A STORÏAU ERAILL. The title story, 'Y Llwybr Arian' *(The Silver Path)*, pictures for us a primitive society, though the characters are given names sufficiently contemporary, Olwen, Arthur and Idris. By killing a lion Arthur becomes a hero and wins Olwen's admiration and the jealousy of Idris. But Arthur is more than a killer: he has a deep sense of the mystery of nature, of the oaktree and the sea— and of life. He marvels at the fair goddess, the Moon, and the silver path over the sea. Idris by killing a lioness gains honour and Olwen's devotion. Arthur ventures out on the silver path. He for Tegla represents the spiritually sensitive in all ages. He proclaims a similar truth in what is possibly the best known of his stories, 'Yr Epaddyn Rhyfedd' *(The Strange Apeman)*, which in an English version has found its way into more than one collection of English-language stories from Wales. This takes us back to a simian-human society in the distant haze of our pre-history, to a generation of apemen among whom has appeared an apeman of superior intelligence and imagination who tries to teach them new skills and who in danger can lead them to safety. He also responds with joy to the beauty of the sunset. The other apemen tear him to pieces. The huge beast that threatens them devours his flesh, and this enables the others to escape. At the end we are told that this apeman was the first man and that the second man did not appear until a myriad years had gone by. The tale is all the more effective for being told with economy. Both these stories seem to presuppose an evolutionary understanding of human development but there is emphasis on a sense of wonder in the presence of beauty. Whether the strange apeman was meant to prefigure Christ is a question which could be debated with considerable heat.

One of the best of Tegla's parable-stories is 'Samuel Jones yr Hendre yn Diolch am ei Gynhaeaf' *(The Harvest Thanksgiving of Samuel Jones, Yr Hendre)* which contrasts the complacent piety of the rich farmer Mr. Herbert, y Fron, with the agonizing faith of Samuel Jones whose life is an unequal struggle against all that is hostile to the tiller of the soil. He decorates the country chapel with thorns and brambles and weeds and they become for him the splendid garment of the Lord. The story is a protest against any facile interpretation of the providential governance of the universe and like *The Strange Apeman* is all the more effective because of its measure of restraint. This is more than can be said for 'Yr Arwr' *(The Hero)* which is an attack on the glorification of soldiers in periods of war hysteria. It pictures the growth of a young ruffian who becomes a soldier without any noble motive and thereby qualifies for posthumous recognition as a war hero.

Two stories are about the life of the minister. One, 'Y Parchedig John Pwlpudedig Jones yn adolygu ei Gofiant ei Hun' *(The Reverend J. Pulpiteer Jones reviews a Biography of Himself)*, is at the same

74

time a skit on the once traditional pious ministerial biography and a fantasy on the nature of
the after-life. We see Jones sitting on the shore of
the Tranquil Lake in Beyond the Veil. Like other
departed souls he has to walk around the lake
three times 'in order to get used to the idea of
eternity before a man's final destiny is decided'.
He sees a woman reading a book and then
flinging it with revulsion into the lake and
fleeing. Jones retrieves the book and sees that it
is a biography of himself by his 'friend' the
Reverend R. Cordeddwr (Twister) Williams. He
finds it full of pious falsehoods conveyed in an
affected and hackneyed style; and in the handling
of all this Tegla treats us to some of his most
delicious ridicule. The biographer says nothing
of Nansi'r Hafod whom Jones jilted, and handles
with discreet reticence the circumstances in
which he married the well-to-do Elin of Y Faerdre
to whose hand the biographer himself had vainly
aspired. The girl who threw the book into the
lake turns out to be Nansi. After a vain attempt
to drown herself in the lake she sees Jones and
embraces him. Elin also appears, looking for her
own true love who is not Pulpiteer but Twister.
Jones's second wife, whose companionship on
earth was unbearable, is also on this purgatorial
lakeside, 'but', as her husband remarks with what
seems to me to be less than Christian concern,
'she will be an old maid here anyway.' Her
ultimate fate seems unsure; and Jones himself is
in no hurry to taste eternity so long as he has
Nansi, though we are told that there are some
who are nearing the conclusion of their triple
rounding of the lake and have the brightness of
the end in their eyes. The story is a good example

of Tegla's inventive imagination. 'Yr Oedfa Fawr' *(The Great Preaching Meeting)* is less notable. It describes a prodigiously successful preaching service in which the preacher is one of the rising stars in the Nonconformist firmament. Among his hearers is a forgotten old man, himself in former days a preacher who knew how it felt to sway a great congregation. In the course of the sermon the young preacher quotes a verse which had been the text used by the old man in one of his great meetings, and after hearing those words the forgotten pulpit veteran loses himself in the memory of that triumph. The narrative carries with it more than a suggestion of the vanity of this transient kind of 'great' preaching.

A more slapstick attack on worldly religiosity is the story of 'Meri Ann' *(Mary Ann)*. The lowly washerwoman who is the titular heroine knows nothing of religion; but she is persuaded to go to a superior Prayer Meeting of fashionable ladies which is described with some grotesquerie. She has her own very different encounter with the holy and the heavenly—without losing her innocent awe of grand ladies.

'Weindio'r Cloc' *(Winding the Clock)* is the most unpretentious story in the volume. It introduces us to a newly married couple in rural Wales. Mali dusts the clock so that John can undertake for the first time the task of winding it, the clock given to him on his wedding day by his father who had received it on his own wedding day from his father. The ceremony of winding it signifies that John is master in his own house, but it is balanced by an equally significant rite when John transfers

his wages to Mali's care. Years later, just after
John's death, Mali, before going to bed, tells their
son William not to forget to wind the clock; but
when she comes down in the morning the clock
has stopped.

RHYFEDD O FYD *(It's a Strange World)* is a diverting
collection of cautionary tales or ironical essays of
satirical intent. 'Ar Hanner Nos' *(At Midnight)*
explores the possibility of a waxworks show for
Wales with comic suggestions ending up with the
Church as the Sleeping Beauty, but also with the
hint of a wistful hope that the Prince may come
to awaken her with a kiss. 'Hunangofiant Pender-
fyniad' *(The Autobiography of a Resolution)* is a perfect
piece of sustained irony detailing the adventures
of a pious resolution proposed and passed in
denominational assemblies, taking us from its
birth in a train conversation to its arrival at the
'Salvage' centre. Other shafts directed against the
plight of Welsh Christianity are 'Breuddwyd
Robert Jones' *(Robert Jones's Dream)* which ridicules
the dream of uniting denominations on the
principle of incorporating features of each in
some composite structure; 'Oedfa Radio' *(Radio
Service)* in which there is some arch ragging of
radio preachers and of homes in which the
broadcast Welsh service is turned on in order to
impress the neighbours; 'Urdd B.P.C.' *(The B.M.F.
League)*, a delicious masterpiece of irony which
lures the reader on with admirable finesse until
the interdenominational League's true nature is
revealed with the disclosure of the meaning of
the mysterious initials; 'Ein Pobl Ni' *(Our People)*,
a shrewd and twinkling prod at the tendency of

the Welsh denominations to take somewhat overweening pride in the eisteddfodic and other successes of their own members; and 'Y Sêr yn eu Graddau' *(The Stars in their Courses*—but the Welsh word for 'courses' here more usually means 'degrees'), which makes rather laboured game of the fact that those denominations in which hierarchical titles have been rejected tend all too often to give prominence to their ministers' academic degrees. This last piece ends powerfully with stark mention of the qualifications of the apostle Paul—'I bear in my body the marks of the Lord Jesus'—and it is a pity that he spoils this a little by yielding to the temptation to say that this is the degree of Jesus College.

The National Eisteddfod and the Gorsedd of the Bards also come in for their share of playful banter as in 'Anhunedd John Jones' *(John Jones's Insomnia)* where their relationship to Wales and to each other is amusingly caricatured in a mischievous parable. In 'Masharŵns' *(Mushrooms)* the sight of a number of specimens of the fungus named in the title leads to thoughts about the Bardic Gorsedd and reflections on the oddity of the fact that so many chapelgoers who reject ceremonial in church worship delight in the Gorsedd rites. Tegla then notes that the glory of the mushroom is shortlived and says this is also true of the Welsh fervour in some places where the Eisteddfod is held and of the fame of many of the winning poems.

Then there are utterances in which Tegla's concern for the Welsh language and cultural heritage is evident. 'Chwadal y Sais' *(As the*

Englishman says) treats the matter lightly and yet shows real feeling about the unnecessary use by Welsh speakers of English expressions to the neglect of vivid modes of speech long available in their native tongue. 'Y Tro Olaf' *(The Last Time)* is a more rollicking exposure of the corruption of spoken Welsh. The dialogue between a Welsh boy of today and the ghost of his great-great-grandfather would be uproariously funny if it were not for the sobering impact of the degeneracy not only of speech but also of values apparent in the lad's remarks. In 'Noson Lawen' we share the depression of a sick old man who loves the Welsh inheritance and is dismayed to see it threatened by a meretricious cultural cosmopolitanism; but we see him also comforted and encouraged when he sees young leaders of Welsh popular culture adapting their methods to meet the challenge of the age. The message of 'Hen Ŷd y Wlad' *(Old Country Corn)* is that a culture will flourish insofar as it assimilates new influences without forfeiting its identity. Yet Tegla's cultural patriotism does not prevent him in the remaining piece in this volume, 'Simon y Selot' *(Simon the Zealot)*, from excoriating Plaid Cymru for trying to raise money by running a competition. He likens the promoters of this little idea to Simon the Zealot and Judas Iscariot whom he depicts with perhaps more verve than justice as the financial wizards of the original Jesus movement.

VII

Urged on by his children Tegla wrote the book of memoirs, GYDA'R BLYNYDDOEDD *(With the Years)*, which appeared in 1952. Having shown his disdain for the conventional biographies of ministers he may have preferred to write his own rather than to leave the task to someone else. What he has given us is by no means a book of confessions and only in part can it be described as a 'spiritual' autobiography. He prefers on the whole to speak of background, forbears, circumstances and those whose lives, for good or for ill, touched his. He gives us much information about the region where he was born and reared and some about his more immediate ancestry. We also hear of childhood experiences which made their marks in his memory and helped to mould his life. The book has one undeniable virtue: the more the reader reads on, the more interested he becomes. We meet a wide range of characters as we hear of Tegla's school days, his time as pupil teacher and lay preacher, his years at College and his various ministries. In his judgements he sometimes seems to see either black or white, as when he recalls his period at Didsbury College, but for the most part he shows a mellow magnanimity, as in his treatment of the conflict at Tre-garth on questions of Biblical criticism. The work will be of value to future historians as well as to all who are interested in Tegla's development as thinker and artist.

As much may be said also of many of the essays in GYDA'R HWYR *(At Eventide)*. Here again we have some of his recollections and some appreciations of men whom he loved or respected, like his friend and fellow-minister Evan Roberts and Robert Richards the scholar and member of Parliament. We are introduced to a number of characters ranging from the conscientious and fastidious simpletons Isaac and Elin to the pretty boy Idris who was lured into a life of dissipation and prostitution and whose mutilated body was found in the Manchester Ship Canal. We also hear of Tegla's two literary 'discoveries'—that Daniel Owen the novelist as a boy, according to the testimony of a very old lady who had been a childhood friend of his, was an avid and re-sourceful perpetrator of practical jokes and that Islwyn's much admired poem 'Seren Heddwch' *(Star of Peace)* was a translation of a poem in English by a Scotswoman, Jane Cross Simpson. Tegla has his own view also of Ann Griffiths the hymnwriter and mystic in his essay 'Ym Maldwyn' *(In Montgomeryshire)*. It is a passage which arouses regret that he did not write more in the way of literary criticism. He has been visiting Plas Cyfronnydd with its home for retarded girls:

I wonder whether Ann Griffiths could have found joy in looking after an institution like this School for retarded children in the name of the Lord, the Man who said,— 'Suffer the little children to come unto me'? If she had done so, she would not have continued to gaze like the eagle into the eye of the sun, but she would have found its light about her feet, to show her with every step the step to be taken next. She yearned to carry the cross and to count it a crown, her own cross, not the crosses of life's stricken ones. That is why I feel somewhat uneasy about her future if she had lived—that the steam might have burst the engine, not driven it on.

But who knows? There are saints like Teresa in whom Martha and Mary have been united.

There are naturally some personal reminiscences in the collections of sermons, radio talks and articles published by Tegla. The most moving of these is the description in Y FOEL FAEN of the accident suffered by his father in his work as quarryman and the quiet courage with which he bore the weakness and deformity it brought.

VIII

Tegla Davies is the author also of a considerable body of expository prose in which he sought to declare the beliefs and values which were for him of the essence of Christianity. Not all of his writings in the way of instruction and edification are of equal value. Some were done in the service of his denomination and some in fulfilment of his undertakings as columnist or broadcaster. Others were originally prepared for delivery as sermons but retain their value in their published form—rather more than most printed sermons, for all too frequently messages delivered with overwhelming effect before a congregation are dull and lifeless in print, whereas Tegla, whose pulpit virtues were virtues of thought and style, expresses himself as limpidly and as persuasively today on paper as he ever did before an audience. This is not to say that every illustrative anecdote will impress a critical reader in the same way as it may have impressed a congregation of humble hearers. For me the finest parts of Tegla's sermons are those in which he expounds the text for he was a well-read scholar and believed that a text should be rightly understood and not used as a mere peg on which to hang the preacher's sometimes misbegotten opinions. Perhaps the best example of this is the title sermon of the volume Y DYHEAD *(The Yearning* or *Panting)* on the text which tells of the hart (or, properly, the hind) panting after the water-brooks. Among the richest and most reverberative of his sermons

are those on the New Creation in the same
volume and on the rejected Stone in Y Ffordd
(The Way). Most of his sermons are clearly
purpose-built, and even the illustrations illustrate.

Those who have commented on Tegla's theological outlook have had, of course, to concede that
in his early years as a minister he insisted that the
Bible must be understood in the light of historical
criticism and of modern knowledge, though he
never said that either of these had reached a
static perfection; but some have been at pains to
show that in his emphasis on the holiness and
righteousness of God and on the centrality of
Christ he was nevertheless a proclaimer of the
essence of Christian orthodoxy. Thus Islwyn
Ffowc Elis, who has done more than most to give
Tegla his due honour, says, *Although he was one of
the early apostles of Biblical Criticism in Wales and still
continues to pierce the stout walls of tradition and doctrine
to reach the Jesus of history, he is not a liberal in his theology.
In the light he has on the Work and Person of Christ he is
entirely Evangelical . . . The truth is that Tegla Davies's
belief in Christ the crucified and risen Saviour is deeper and
more incandescent than the belief of many who accept the
verbal inspiration of the Bible.* W. Eifion Powell sees
liberalism and evangelical doctrine, partly traditional and partly neo-orthodox, elbowing each
other in Tegla's thought: *It would be untrue to say that
he halts between two opinions, but the general scheme, as well
as many particular features, of the liberal theology appealed
to him, while at the same time he continued to keep tight hold
of the certitude of the Christian revelation as that certitude
has been emphasised in the theology of Karl Barth and as
Tegla himself was acquainted with it in the revivalist*

tradition of the Methodist Church. Dafydd Jenkins sees a development in Tegla from one phase to another: *As far as I can see,* he writes, *the prophet's development has not been traced by anybody, and although I am not qualified to trace it myself, I am convinced that there has been development and tend to believe that it was in the years during and following the Second War that the great development took place. To judge from the selection he made for the* BLODEUGERDD FEIBLAIDD *(Biblical Anthology) of the Book Club in 1939, Tegla at that time was a liberal Nonconformist of a not uncommon type, but in his later writing he was pretty critical of every denominational rut.* But he admits that there had been preliminary flashes of the prophetic fire before that.

All this goes to confirm my suspicion that theological discussion has been too long bedevilled by this facile placing of the terms 'liberal' and 'evangelical' in opposition to each other. Two truths about Tegla's outlook need to be brought out. One is that he accepted both 'creation' and 'evolution' as complementary aspects of the origin and condition of life and of humanity. In a sermon published in Y DYHEAD as late as the year before he died he says—in my view somewhat extravagantly—that Charles Darwin was probably the greatest man in the world in his own age. Elsewhere in that volume, in the sermon on the New Creation, he speaks of the grades of being—plants, animals, mankind and the children of the New Creation in Christ—and accepts the principle that a creature can emerge from one grade to another. He points to the apeman who became man ruled by reason and understanding and to the blessedness of those made new in Christ and filled with love and faith. No doubt there is oversimplification here but we can be sure that this doctrine provides the key to Tegla's stories of the Silver Path and the Strange Apeman. The other truth is that he conceives of the divine glory of Christ in moral and not ontological terms and so parts company with the traditional creeds and fiercely defended orthodoxies old and new. In the sermon on Believing in the Son in the same volume he makes it clear that it is the forgiving love of Jesus Christ that constitutes his Divine Sonship and that prevails over death. For Tegla these two truths belong together. They are brought together in the short book DECHRAU'R DAITH *(Beginning the Journey)* written for young candidates for church membership and published in 1943. There he speaks of plants as a comparatively low form of life and says that the emergence of birds and animals is a new act of creation. The appearance of man on earth is another re-creation. A yet higher form of life is the life of the Christian, the life of love, and Tegla applies to this new creation the teaching that to see the Kingdom of God we must be born again. This life, he says, is God's life, and Jesus Christ came into the world to show man what God's life is and to enable us to receive it. A logical inference from this, though Tegla does not make it explicit, is that Jesus was the first to live this Christian life. Tegla does indeed say that what made Jesus different from others is that his enemies failed to get him to hate them, so that even on the Cross he could pray that they might be forgiven.

The little book says nothing about the incarnation of a pre-existent Being, and it would seem that such a notion meant little to Tegla. In his sermon on the Stone he gives his own interpretation of one of the famous declarations in the Prologue to the Fourth Gospel, 'All things were made through him, and without him was not anything made that was made'. He says that this means not that the Lord Jesus is the Creator, but that the creation is done through him in the sense that 'the fundamental principles of God's creation are the principles of the character of Jesus Christ'. DECHRAU'R DAITH is also virtually silent about the doctrine of the Trinity. It is only in connection with baptism in the chapter on the sacraments that mention is made of 'the name of the Father and of the Son and of the Holy Spirit', and it is only in this passage that the Spirit is named at all. Eifion Powell, though affirming Tegla's sure grasp of the basic truths of the Christian faith, remarks that only one of his sermons is devoted to the Holy Spirit and that Tegla like Paul had difficulty in distinguishing between the Holy Spirit and the Spirit of Christ. It should be added that the volume Y FFORDD, in addition to containing the discourse on the power of the Holy Spirit under the title 'Tystion' (*Witnesses*), has a prefatory word to the effect that the dominant note of the whole collection is the proclamation of the Risen Christ as the Son of God *'according to the spirit of holiness'* (italicised by Tegla). He evidently does not regard the Spirit as a distinct divine Person. It is the springlike burgeoning of Christian zeal in a young heart and a young movement, a widening of vision, a cleansing of character, a harnessing of spiritual aspirations.

87

Tegla Davies never undertook to systematise his theology, but in Y SANHEDRIN he handled some of the inevitable themes in the form of discussions at a time of war between a minister, a schoolmaster, a conscientious objector, a bank clerk, a farmer and a shopkeeper. The aim is stimulus rather than finality and the aim is amply achieved; but although Tegla's voice can be heard behind his puppets and with persuasive power behind some of them, and especially the minister and the conscientious objector, we cannot attribute any of the opinions without reserve to Tegla's own convictions. Yet knowing him in his other utterances we can be sure that it is he who is speaking when we hear that in heaven there is boundless suffering, for God himself suffers as he beholds the condition of the world, and that in hell there is no suffering because there is no sensitivity; that the real meaning of 'miracle' is 'action which mediates a revelation of the inner character of God' and that the supreme miracle is the Christian life, the life of the Church as the new community, a miracle greater even than the Resurrection which is a manifestation of the truth that the character of the supreme power in the universe is like the character of the Crucified; that all the emphasis of the Gospel is upon being born from above and that just as man emerged from the anthropoid— with the promise of the coming humanity manifesting itself at first in one or two marvellously gifted individuals—so is the higher man called 'Christian' emerging through faith; and that although our ecclesiastical systems and secular civilisations may pass away the Architect is calmly and unhurriedly working out his purpose and building the eternal Church which is above all ages.

It would seem therefore that evil for Tegla is imperfection, incompleteness, the dross and the waste that are part of the process of growth; but he does not explore the problem. Now and again he ruefully and even jocularly makes passing mention of the Devil. He says in Y FOEL FAEN that the god of Darkness opposed to the god of Light in ancient Persia entered into Old Testament religion as the Devil and pertinently asks whether those who think of him as a personal being suppose that he is omniscient and omnipotent and omnipresent. He mentions him also in a sermon in GORCHFYGU'R BYD only to dismiss him as a negative concept. But he does not shut his eyes to the evils of the age and many of the essays in Y FOEL FAEN and AR DDISBEROD are concerned with them: the craze for easy satisfactions and degrading thrills, the willingness to confuse spirituality with external grandeur, the making of pretexts to escape from obligations and of compromises to evade principles, the clinging to old ideas and practices, the abandonment of truth and responsibility in the media of communication, the cult of brash pulpit oratory, the misplaced emphasis on by-products of Christianity rather than on the Gospel itself, drift, complacency and worldliness in the churches, the tendency of some Christians to retreat from the world into their own inward looking organisations and of others to look for some apocalyptic intervention in the future and of others to trim their faith to make it more acceptable to the world and of others again to content themselves

with something easier than the Gospel such as
biblical literalism or subservience to the state. It
is very largely these diagnostic discourses that
have earned for Tegla the epithet 'prophet'.

As he seeks to confront the world's evils he
points to the spiritual resources that are mightier
than they. One is the sense of God, the theme
of one of his best known essays, 'Headroom', in
which he speaks of men such as Abraham and
Moses whose world was geographically very
small but spiritually very spacious and likens
their blessedness to that of an old blacksmith
who worked in a tiny roofless smithy but boasted
of its headroom. And this, of course, is for him
related to the glory of Christ who, lifted up
from the earth, draws all unto him. Integral to
his Christianity also is the affirmation of the
equality and unity of all mankind and the
power of love to overcome evil and death. He
proclaims also the new man in Christ Jesus as
the supreme species, the Christian species, which
is the goal of the development of life on our
earth. It is the emphasis on Christ as the uniquely
perfect expression in history of the character of
God that has led some interpreters to associate
him with 'orthodoxy' so-called, either in one of
its traditional forms or in relation to its twentieth-
century recrudescence; but his theological pre-
suppositions are very different from those of
Thomists and Calvinists past and present. On
the other hand, he is not to be ranked with those
who regard Jesus of Nazareth in merely human
terms as one of the greatest, or even the greatest,
of the saints, heroes and benefactors of mankind.
His thought, in any case, deserves to be known

for its intrinsic value. It has affinities to contemporary process theology.

One result of his concern to preserve the unsullied moral perfection of Christ was to lead him at times to exalt him above our human conflict and so to make unreal his involvement in the issues of his own age and his own people. One of his sermons in GORCHFYGU'R BYD argues that Jesus of Nazareth was detached from the political and social struggles of his own age, that he had nothing to say about the injustices for which Tiberius, Herod and Pilate were responsible, that he did not denounce slavery or the oppression by the rich of the poor, and that he refused to take sides in the clash between the Zealots and the supporters of Roman rule in Palestine. Others find good reason for seeing the mission of Jesus in a very different light. It may be that Tegla's own studied aloofness from party political commitment led him to interpret the mission of Jesus in this negative way without giving anything like adequate consideration to the evidence. If so, he would not be the first theologian to read his own character into Christ. In fairness, of course, it must be said that Tegla was consistent and courageous in his witness to the cause of peace.

Tegla's version of the Christian hope is also couched in providential-evolutionary terms. The minister in Y SANHEDRIN rejects John Wesley's belief in the immortality of animals on the grounds that it is only the best manifestations of life that are to be preserved, since God's purpose in the universe is the showing forth of 'the Sons

of God'. In his chapter on the Second Coming in
AR DDISBEROD he says that those who look for a
cataclysmic return of Christ as a future event on
the plane of history are like those contemporaries
of Jesus who demanded of him a 'sign', a dramatic
piece of showmanship to establish his credentials.
Tegla's own teaching is that the Second Coming
is already with us. It is to be seen in the serenity
of humble folk in their afflictions and in the
innocence of little children. Christ is with them,
with his little ones. And, adds Tegla,

*I believe I see this increasing until little by little it grows and
spreads and at last the name of Jesus is exalted throughout
the world. And then with his triumph the end will come as he
presents the Kingdom to his Father so that God shall be all in
all. Today he is rejected as of old by those who hold sway in
world and church, but he is revealed to 'little ones' every day
of their lives. I am content with this coming. It is He who
has the power to conquer.*

I would not deny Tegla his hope even though
the 'little ones' are being threatened more and
more by a civilisation which promotes very
different values and is armed with terrifying
powers of coercion, corruption and control.

IX

Tegla Davies is a greatly gifted writer and his gifts
are held together, not always harmoniously, in
an unique combination. He is a compulsive
moralist whose work nevertheless has given
delight to children; a searing satirist for whom the
central truth of our human existence is love; an
enchanter who can conjure up imaginary realms
and who is also a prophet called to denounce the
evils of his time. A penetrating and original
thinker, he could have become a notable theologian if he had presented his teachings system-
atically instead of leaving his readers to piece
them together out of his discursive sermons and
digressive essays. Nevertheless he has left us
some remarkable insights and an emphasis which
ought to present a challenge both to our retro-
gressive literalists and to those who would reduce
the Christ-event to a mere mirage in the daunting
wastes of secular history.

As novelist as well as theologian Tegla just
missed doing justice to himself. GŴR PEN Y BRYN
had all the makings of a great novel, a magnificent
theme, style, background, passages and episodes
of undeniable merit, but it needed more space,
more detail and deeper and more individualised
characterisation than were given to it; and of
course the didactic intention should have been
less intrusive. HUNANGOFIANT TOMI reaches classic
status and comes nearer to being a novel though
it is much shorter and GYDA'R GLANNAU too is

93

more successful though as a piece of satire it aims less high. Tegla's articles and discourses also somehow fall short of qualifying as literary essays. Some partake of the nature of memoirs and others of sermons; while those in RHYFEDD O FYD, though genuine literary essays of the satirical kind and for the most part deliciously wrought, are directed against victims too specific and lose, even for those who agree with them, that measure of charm which endears the best humorous essays.

The 'entertainment value' of NEDW and Y DOCTOR BACH is almost as high as that of HUNANGOFIANT TOMI, and the stories ' 'Rhen Nedw' and 'Torri'r Saboth' are masterpieces. Equally above all question is the quality of three stories in Y LLWYBR ARIAN, 'Yr Epaddyn Rhyfedd', 'Samuel Jones yr Hendre yn Diolch am ei Gynhaeaf' and 'Meri Ann'. All the episodes in TIR Y DYNEDDON, despite inconsistencies and the pointing of an occasional moral, are beautiful and moving, and the book is a triumph of the art of fairy tale. HEN FFRINDIAU in its quaint and comic way is also a masterwork, and here the moralist exercises a self-effacing restraint and we ourselves are left to stage our own existential revolution and find ourselves in safe hands. There is much also in RHYS LLWYD Y LLEUAD and STORI SAM that we should not want to lose, and, of course, in GŴR PEN Y BRYN, such as the unforgettable narration of the crisis of the sheepdogs.

W. J. Gruffydd has summed up the three domi-nant interests which in his view constitute Tegla's distinctive contribution to literature. One

94

is his irrepressible delight in the little world of
the child, especially of course in the context of
the Welsh country life he had known and loved.
Another is his desire to express the meaning of
human life through the symbols conjured up by
his imagination, an enterprise in which he did
not wholly succeed, despite much that is delectable in such works as TIR Y DYNEDDON and
STORI SAM. And the third is his belief in the
possibility and indeed the necessity of regener-
ation, of being born again. Gruffydd seems to be
thinking chiefly of the conversions and semi-
conversions and pseudo-conversions in GŴR PEN
Y BRYN, GYDA'R GLANNAU and the half-ironic
picture of the after-life of J. Pwlpudedig Jones;
but we have seen that Tegla contemplates also
the transfiguration of humanity into the divinely
redeemed and redemptive life pioneered by
Jesus of Nazareth and brought to completion by
God's love in the living Christ. If in our reading
of Tegla we have missed this, we have missed all.

In all his work we have a sense that our lives are
part of a wondrous miracle, an amazing ad-
venture. All our existences have meaning and
purpose. He disdains all escapism: STORI SAM was
written, despite its confusions, to exorcise it. We
live in the here and now and the surest wisdom
is to be seen in the simple trust of little children,
the grateful endurance of the poor and the down-
trodden, the smile of God's little ones—Lisi Bach
and Mathew Tomos—even as death claims them.
But it would be a mistake to assume that Tegla
offers an otherworldly haven. His hope springs
from his faith in the goal set before us, the
consummation of all life in the Christ Life

towards which all the evolving phases of God's creative activity are directed. To serve that end is to live and to conquer death. Tegla's magical power as myth-maker is used not to transport us to a dream world of easy happiness but rather to show us the meaning of the present existence so incredibly bestowed upon us.

Select Bibliography

E. TEGLA DAVIES

HUNANGOFIANT TOMI, Evan Thomas, Bangor, 1912.

LLESTRI'R TRYSOR (ed. with D. Tecwyn Evans), Evan Thomas, Bangor, 1914.

TIR Y DYNEDDON, Hughes a'i Fab, Wrexham, 1921.

NEDW, Hughes a'i Fab, Cardiff, 1922.

Y GREAL SANCTAIDD, Hughes a'i Fab, Wrexham, 1922.

GŴR PEN Y BRYN, Hughes a'i Fab, Wrexham, 1922.

BRANWEN FERCH LLYR, Hughes a'i Fab, Wrexham, 1923.

RHYS LLWYD Y LLEUAD, Hughes a'i Fab, Wrexham, 1925.

IESU O NASARETH, Hughes a'i Fab, Wrexham, 1927.

HEN FFRINDIAU, Hughes a'i Fab, Wrexham, 1927.

Y DOCTOR BACH, Hughes a'i Fab, Wrexham, 1930.

Y LLWYBR ARIAN A STORÏAU ERAILL, Hughes a'i Fab, Wrexham, 1934.

STORI SAM, Hughes a'i Fab, Wrexham, 1938.

Y FLODEUGERDD FEIBLAIDD, Y Clwb Llyfrau Cymraeg, 1939.

GYDA'R GLANNAU, Llyfrau'r Dryw, Llandybïe, 1941.

DECHRAU'R DAITH, Llyfrau'r Dryw, Llandybïe, 1943.

GORCHFYGU'R BYD, Llyfrau Pawb, Denbigh, 1944.

Y SANHEDRIN, Y Clwb Llyfrau Cymraeg, 1945.

RHYFEDD O FYD, Gwasg y Brython, 1950.

Y FOEL FAEN, Gwasg y Brython, Liverpool, 1951.

GYDA'R BLYNYDDOEDD, Gwasg y Brython, Liverpool, 1952.

AR DDISBEROD, Gwasg y Brython, Liverpool, 1954.

GYDA'R HWYR, Gwasg y Brython, Liverpool, 1957.

Y FFORDD, Gwasg y Brython, 1959.

YR HEN GWPAN CYMUN, Gwasg y Brython, 1961.

Y DYHEAD, Llyfrau'r Dryw, 1966.

THE MASTER OF PEN Y BRYN, translation by Nina Watkins of Gŵr Pen y Bryn, Christopher Davies, Llandybïe, 1975.

Biographical

Ethall, Huw, Tegla, Tŷ John Penry, 1980.

Critical

Elis, Islwyn Ffowc, Dirgelwch Tegla (Eisteddfod Genedlaethol), 1977.

Elis, Islwyn Ffowc (ed.), Edward Tegla Davies: Llenor a Phroffwyd, Gwasg y Brython, Liverpool, 1956. The volume contains a foreword by Arfor Tegla Davies and contributions by Gwilym R. Tilsley, D. Tecwyn Evans, R. W. Davies, David Thomas, Dyddgu Owen, D. Tecwyn Lloyd and the editor.

Gruffydd, W. J., 'Nodiad arbennig ar Mr. Tegla Davies', in Y Llenor, xx, pp. 148–151.

Jenkins, Dafydd, 'Tegla', in Taliesin 42, pp. 9–24.

Jones, R. M., Llenyddiaeth Gymraeg 1936–1972, Christopher Davies, Llandybïe, pp. 229–233.

Jones, T. Gwynn, 'Tegla', in YR EURGRAWN, cxxvii, pp. 95–101.

Lloyd, D. Tecwyn, 'Chwyldro Tegla' in Y GENHINEN, xviii, pp. 32–41.

Lloyd, D. Tecwyn, SAFLE'R GERBYDRES, Gwasg Gomer, Llandysul, 1970, pp. 164–176.

Powell, W. Eifion, 'Diwinyddiaeth Tegla' in DIWINYDDIAETH, xxxi, pp. 66–75.

Ruddock, Gilbert, 'Gŵr Pen y Bryn', in BARN 47, pp. 314–5, 48, pp. 339–40, 49, p. 23.

The Author

PENNAR DAVIES is a native of Aberpennar (Mountain Ash) in the Cynon Valley. Educated at first locally and afterwards in the Universities of Wales (at Cardiff), Oxford (as research student at Balliol) and Yale (in the Graduate School) and trained for the Christian ministry at Mansfield College, Oxford, he spent a little over three years in a pastoral charge at Cardiff before becoming a theological college tutor in Church History. His fields of research had been in English literature (John Bale, Edmund Spenser and George Chapman), but Welsh and theological interests inevitably supervened. Through his membership of the Cadwgan literary group he met Rosemarie Wolff who became his wife. He has served in theological colleges at Bangor, Brecon, Swansea and Aberystwyth. His publications include several volumes of verse, three novels, short stories, a confessional diary and critical, theological and historical studies on such themes as the Divine Absence, the consciousness of Jesus, the theology of Spirit, early Welsh mythology and religion, Dissent in Wales, theories of church-state relationship and modern Welsh literary figures. He has contested parliamentary elections in the interest of Plaid Cymru, edited the first Welsh tribute volume (to Saunders Lewis) and published a brief biography of Gwynfor Evans.

This Edition,
designed by Jeff Clements,
is set in Monotype Spectrum 12 Didot on 13 point
and printed on Basingwerk Parchment by
Qualitex Printing Limited, Cardiff

It is limited to 1000 copies of which this is

Copy No. 0609

British Library Cataloguing in Publication Data

Davies, Pennar
  E. Tegla Davies.—(Writers of Wales, ISSN 0141-5050)
  I. Davies, Edward Tegla—Criticism and interpretation
  I. Title II. Series
  891.6′6′8208   PB2298.D/

  ISBN 0-7083-0842-2